THE   REAL

CHILLI

COOKBOOK

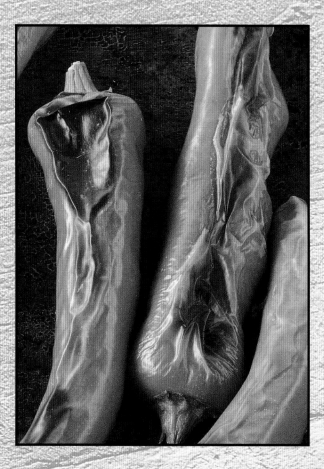

THE REAL
CHILLI
COOKBOOK

THE ULTIMATE
HOT AND SPICY EXPERIENCE

M A R J I E L A M B E R T

APPLE

DEDICATION

Dedicated to my friends who work in newsrooms across the
country and who share my passion for writing.

A QUINTET BOOK

Published by the Apple Press
6 Blundell Street
London N7 9BH

ISBN 1-85076-700-9

This book was designed and produced by
Quintet Publishing Limited
6 Blundell Street
London N7 9BH

CREATIVE DIRECTOR: *Richard Dewing*
DESIGNER: *Simon Balley*
SENIOR EDITOR: *Laura Sandelson*
EDITOR: *Barbara Croxford*
PHOTOGRAPHER: *David Armstrong*

Typeset in Great Britain by
Central Southern Typesetters, Eastbourne
Manufactured in Malaysia by
C.H. Colour Scan SDN BHD
Printed in Singapore by
Star Standard Industries (Pte) Ltd

AUTHOR ACKNOWLEDGMENTS
With thanks to Terry, who hopes he never smells cumin again; to Laura at Quintet;
and to my colleagues at the *Sun-Sentinel*, who boldly tasted what no one had tasted before.

Contents

Introduction

The history of chilli has as many twists and tangents as a tale by a champion story-teller. And like any tall tale, it is impossible to sort out the facts, exaggerations, embroidered truths, competing claims and downright lies about chilli. Who made the first pot of chilli, and when? There are stories of meat-and-chilli stews dating to the 16th century, and there were probably 16th-century men who bragged of eating chilli so hot that a week later, their breath could still boil water. But it wasn't until well into the 19th century that chilli became institutionalized, a staple of the American frontier. Why? It was a hardy food of non-perishable ingredients that were easily transported, a simple concoction of wild chillies, animal fat and dried beef or hunter's game. Long hours of simmering softened the toughest, driest meats, and the chillies disguised any rancid flavour.

Lavanderas, *Mexican laundresses* who followed the Mexican Army across the Rio Grande and later served Texas and U.S. militiamen, simmered the tough, stringy meat of the scrawny cattle and deer that grazed along the U.S./Mexican border. Chuckwagon cooks boiled scraps of meat and fat with chillies, onions and oregano from the "spice groves" that they planted along the cattle trails. Frontiersmen and gold miners stuffed their saddlebags with "jerky" (sun-dried meat) that had been pounded with fat and chillies, then boiled the meat to make a spicy dinner. And the chilli queens of San Antonio sold bowls of chilli from their stalls in the city's Military Plaza.

None of those unappetizing beginnings would have predicted success. Given chilli's history, it is amazing it survived into the age of refrigeration, when dried meat and harsh spices were no longer necessities. But instead of fading into obscurity with hardtack and other disagreeable foods, chilli changed with the times. Cooks used fresh, albeit tough cuts of meat. Buffalo and venison chilli became more commonplace, replaced later by beef and pork. When meat was scarce or expensive, they stretched it by adding beans or brown rice to chilli. Canary Islanders who immigrated to Texas brought cumin with them, adding a distinctive flavour that is mandatory among most chilli lovers.

By the late 1800s, chilli was being canned. The San Antonio Chilli Stand – which began with that city's chilli queens – was a feature of the 1893 World's Fair in Chicago. But chilli's popularity really didn't spread outside Texas until the early part of the 20th century. It peaked during the Depression when a bowl of chilli with

Cindy Reed, proud winner of the chilli cook-off in Houston, 1992 and 1993. (Picture courtesy Chili Appreciation Society International)

crackers was one of the heartiest and cheapest meals available in diners. Then World War II brought rationing, and chilli disappeared from many menus.

Its popularity did not revive until the 1960s, when President Johnson's passion for Pedernales River Chilli – made with venison and tomatoes – was widely publicized. Suddenly, chilli's popularity exploded.

Today, chilli is one of America's most popular dishes. In 1977, chilli was named the official State Dish of Texas, and a contingent of chilliheads regularly lobbies for it to be named the official dish of the United States. Chilli has been influenced by Mexican cooking but it is an all-American dish. The Chili Appreciation Society International and a splinter group, the International Chili Society, hold frequent chilli cook-offs that draw thousands of people. There is now a chilli cook-off circuit, much like the beauty pageant circuit, where cooks compete in smaller contests to win the right to compete in the big ones.

What began as a simple dish has assumed almost mythical status, boosted by beer, bragging and the cook's secret ingredient, a combination that is present almost anywhere chilli is simmering on the fire.

What is chilli? In its purest form, the ingredients are the same that chuckwagon cooks stirred into frontier-era chilli – meat, chillies, onions and spices – although the meat is fresher, and cooks use less fat today. Variety comes from the different cuts of meat and combinations of chillies and spices used. But few people outside Texas make such a basic

chilli. Even in Texas, many cooks use a little tomato sauce for colour and body. Others use masa harina, flour or crumbled crackers to thicken chilli. For cooks who stray beyond basic chilli, beer, lime juice, chopped tomatoes, celery, peppers and a pinch of sugar are common additions. Chilliheads will argue endlessly over whether fresh minced garlic is superior to garlic powder, or whether mild New Mexico chilli powder is superior to California chilli powder.

Beyond those basics, chilli's bold flavours invite creativity. Every passionate chilli cook has a secret ingredient or two. Maybe it is an exotic chilli or chilli powder. Often, however, it is something truly unexpected that adds a mystery note to the symphony of flavours: unsweetened cocoa, coffee, allspice, turmeric, caraway seeds, tequila, corn, olives, finely chopped sun-dried tomatoes, mole powder and roasted garlic are ingredients that show up in a surprising number of chilli pots.

And that doesn't even take into account vegetarian chilli – a spicy vegetable stew that most chilliheads won't recognize.

So what's the perfect chilli recipe? It's all a matter of taste – and what ingredients you have on hand when an urgent craving for chilli strikes. The recipes offered in these pages provide enough variety to suit any mood, any budget, any larder and any palate, from the delicate to the asbestos. But don't limit yourself. If none of these chilli recipes suits your mood or your taste, change them. That's the final ingredient of a great chilli: Creativity.

1

INGREDIENTS AND TECHNIQUES

If you avoid discussions of religion and politics because of the arguments they provoke, stay away from the subject of chilli too. Debates about chilli are fierce, emotional, and highly personal. They often make political or religious arguments sound tame. With or without beans? Kidney suet or canola oil? How coarsely should meat be ground? And are you a sissy if you don't like habanero chillies? Chilliheads believe there is only one true chilli – theirs. And they are not likely to reveal the secret ingredient or technique that makes their chilli superior to all others. But if there were really only one true chilli, there would be no need for chilli cook-offs and chilli cookbooks, and no grounds for bragging. And what fun is chilli-making without bragging? Following is a listing of common and some uncommon chilli ingredients. Some may violate the purity standards of old-line chilliheads, but if you wanted purity, you could passively follow their recipe instead of following your heart – and your palate.

CHILLIES

The chilli – fresh, dried or ground into powder – is the soul of the stew we call chillli.

Chillies – *capsicum* – are native to the Americas and especially to Mexico. Christopher Columbus brought the chilli back from the New World. Now more than 200 varieties grow around the world, and all chilliheads have their favourites. The jalapeño is the most widely available chilli in the U.S., but a chillihead is likely to scoff at the ordinariness of the jalapeño, favouring a serrano, a habanero, or a Thai bird's eye chilli instead. An amateur may brag about how hot he likes his chillies, but a true chillihead will talk about the underlying flavours – the earthy, slightly chocolate flavour of the poblano, the hot-sweet intensity of a cayenne, the nuttiness of a dried cascabel.

Today's cooks have many choices of chillies, which come primarily in three forms: fresh, dried and powdered. Chilli paste is hard to find outside of speciality shops and mail-order sources, but can be used in place of soaked and puréed dried chillies. Canned chillies are also available, but – except for the chipotle chilli and pickled jalapeños (*en escabeche*) – are inferior to other chilli products.

Anaheim

ANAHEIM The Anaheim, also called the California chilli, is the mildest member of the chilli family and a cousin of the New Mexico chilli. It is widely available fresh, probably second to the jalapeño, and is often canned and labelled simply "green chillies". It is pale green, smooth, 10–18 cm/5–7 in long and about 2.5 cm/1 in wide. Dried, it is a deep burgundy colour and is one of the most readily available dried chillies. A mild California chilli powder is made from the Anaheim. In chillis, the Anaheim in any form is usually combined with hotter chillies.

ANCHO See poblano.

ARBOL The chilli de arbol is narrow, about 7.5 cm/3 in long, and bright orange-red. It is very hot. It is most often found dried – sometimes labelled only "dried red chillies" – although other small, hot, dried red chillies such as serranos may also be labelled as chillies de arbol. Pure chilli de arbol powder from Mexico may be found in some very well-stocked grocers.

CALIFORNIA See Anaheim.

Ancho

Arbol

CAYENNE The cayenne is bright red, thin and pointed, 7.5–18 cm/ 3–7 in long. It is extremely hot, yet sweet, with a flavour similar to Thai bird's eye chillies, and is an ingredient in Asian as well as Mexican dishes. It is most familiar dried and ground into cayenne pepper – also called simply red pepper – which will add heat but not much flavour to any dish.

CHIPOTLE See Jalapeño.

HABANERO One of the two hottest chillies in the world, the habanero – its name means from Havana – is most widely used in the Yucatan, but has recently gained popularity among maso-chistic chilliheads in the U.S. The habanero is lantern-shaped and looks like a miniature pepper, just 5 cm/2 in high. Its colour ranges from green to bright orange. It is related to the Scotch Bonnet, an equally hot chilli from the Caribbean. Fresh habaneros are showing up in a growing number of well-stocked grocers or markets, especially those in Hispanic or Caribbean neighbourhoods. Habanero chilli powder and crushed dried habaneros are scarce but can be found.

Dried Habanero

Fresh Habanero

JALAPEÑO The jalapeño, the most widely available fresh chilli in the U.S., is hot, although there are many varieties of chilli that are hotter. Jalapeños are usually 5–7.5 cm/2–3 in long, smooth, glossy, and taper to a rounded end. Although most are sold green, they will turn bright red if left on the bush to ripen. Several raw, chopped and unseeded jalapeños added to chilli will turn up the heat considerably. Roasting jalapeños gives them a marvellous flavour, but they do not need to be roasted. Dried jalapeños are quite scarce. Jalapeño chilli powder is also hard to find. Smoked jalapeños, called *chipotles*, have a wonderful, not at all subtle, smoky flavour and are a delicious addition to chilli. They do not lose any of their heat in the smoking process. Chipotles are available canned in adobo sauce, and can occasionally, be found dried. Tart, pickled jalapeños, called *jalapeños in escabeche*, are more often used as a garnish than an ingredient.

NEGRO See pasilla.

NEW MEXICO This is the chilli that South Westerners rhapsodize about. The New Mexico chilli is a relative of the Anaheim and resembles it in size and shape, but inspires far more passion than its Californian cousin. Don't ever suggest to a chillihead that the Anaheim is in the same league as the beloved New Mexico chilli! It is a light to medium green that darkens to a deep red if left on the bush to ripen. New Mexico green chillies are usually used fresh: the reds are usually dried or roasted and frozen, but it is possible to find fresh New Mexico reds and dried New Mexico greens. In general, the green chilli ranges in heat from moderate to hot – the red is hot.

New Mexico chilli powders are also popular.

PASILLA Also called the *chilli negro*, the pasilla is very dark, purple-black in colour. It is long and slim like the Anaheim, but has wrinkled skin. The flavour is intense and moderately spicy, with just a bit more heat and none of the sweetness of the poblano. It is more readily available dried than fresh. It is often used in commercial chilli powder blends. The dried poblano is sometimes mislabelled as pasilla. A dried poblano (called an *ancho*) is reddish, while the pasilla is brown-black.

POBLANO Although only a moderately spicy chilli, the poblano has a complex, earthy flavour with hints of chocolate. Green chilli stews are usually made with poblanos, which can be used in the large quantities required without making the stew scorchingly hot. In a hot chilli, poblanos are used in combination with hotter chillies. They are usually roasted and peeled. Strips of roasted poblanos, called *rajas*, make delicious garnishes for chilli. In its dried form, the poblano is called *ancho*, although it is sometimes mislabelled as pasilla. The ancho has a rich chilli flavour with hints of raisin, and adds a wonderful note to chillies.

SCOTCH BONNET The incendiary Scotch bonnet is a relative of the habanero and is often confused with its equally fiery cousin. The Scotch bonnet looks like a tiny tam-o'-shanter in colours of green, yellow, orange and red. It is not widely available in the U.K., but a diligent search may find it in a greengrocer or market in a West Indian neighbourhood.

SERRANO Small – about 5 cm/ 2 in long – and thin, the serrano is hotter than the jalapeño but not as hot as the habanero. It is usually sold when glossy green, but it turns red if left on the bush.

Chipotle

Jalapeño

Scotch Bonnet

New Mexico

MISCELLANEOUS CHILLI ITEMS

CHILLI POWDER Chilli powder is a mix of spices that usually includes pure chilli powder, cumin, oregano and garlic powder, but each manufacturer's blend is different. Typically ancho or pasilla chilli powder is used to produce a mild blend. Chilli powder provides an underlying chilli flavour but does not provide heat. It is usually used in combination with cayenne, Tabasco sauce, crushed chilli flakes, or a pure hot chilli powder when a hot chilli is desired. Some spice companies also produce a hotter blend, called hot or Mexican chilli powder, made with hotter chilli powder. This will add moderate heat to a dish. Chilli molido means pure, unspiced chilli powder.

CHILLI FLAKES Also called chilli caribe, these are dried, crushed red chillies, usually New Mexico chillies, and are usually very hot.

TABASCO SAUCE Tabasco sauce is a hot-pepper sauce made from the fermented Tabasco chilli, vinegar, and salt. The Tabasco chilli, from the Mexican state of Tabasco, is a cousin of the cayenne. It is a small, red fiery chilli that is not available commercially. Tabasco sauce has been produced since before the American Civil War, but as chillies have grown in popularity, Tabasco has had competition from a great variety of hot pepper sauces.

▲ *A range of store cupboard ingredients that any serious chilli cook should keep.*

SAFETY PRECAUTIONS FOR COOKING WITH CHILLIES

Chillies' capsaicin content makes them difficult to work with. The capsaicin not only provides the heat on your palate, it will also make your lips, your fingers, your face sting if you get it on your skin. Because capsaicin is not water-soluble, rinsing your skin with water will not decrease the burn and may spread it. If the sting is in your mouth, a dairy product – milk, sour cream, yogurt – or a starchy food such as bread, rice, or beans will help. If it is on your hands or face, soap will help a little; rubbing a little margarine on the area, then washing it off with soap may also help.

Prevention is better, though. Wear latex gloves, the more snug, the better. My sister-in-law, a nurse, gave me some of her surgical gloves – I like them better than other gloves because they are very thin and snug. At a pinch, protect your hand by putting it in a plastic bag before you handle chillies.

Remember that the irritating chilli oils get on knives, work surfaces and dish cloths, and that rinsing with water will not get rid of the capsaicin. The items must be washed thoroughly with soap, preferably in a dishwasher.

Never touch your eyes when you are working with chillies. The burning sensation on your fingers is minimal compared to the pain it will cause in your eyes.

Although roasting the chillies will mellow their heat slightly, they still contain capsaicin, which will burn your fingers. Protect your hands when working with roasted chillies, just as you would with raw chillies.

ROASTING CHILLIES

Roasting chillies gives them a wonderful flavour and takes the edge off their heat. It also allows easy removal of the tough skin on some larger chillies such as Anaheims and poblanos. Smaller chillies, including habanero, serrano and jalapeño, do not need to have their thin skins removed, but may be roasted for the flavour.

Chillies can be roasted whole under the grill and turned (using tongs) during cooking, or cut into two or three large, flat pieces that do not need to be turned. Place the pieces skin side up. The chillies should be 10–15 cm/4–6 in below the grill.

Watch them carefully as they cook. They are ready when the skin is blistered and mostly blackened. They will not cook evenly. If you wait for the skin to be solidly blackened, the flesh may be partly scorched and ruined.

As you remove chillies from the grill, place them in a plastic or paper bag, a covered heatproof bowl or, if you are only roasting one or two chillies, in a foil pouch. Seal the bag or pouch, or put the cover on the bowl. The chillies will steam as they cool, which will make it easy to remove the skins. Leave the chillies for at least 10 minutes. Then peel off the skins. If working with whole chillies, remove the stems and seeds. Remember to wear plastic gloves to protect your hands from chilli juices.

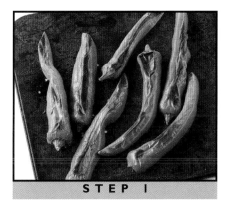

STEP 1

Remove freshly roasted chillies from the grill

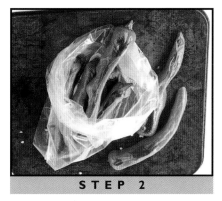

STEP 2

Place chillies in a plastic bag to cool

STEP 3

Peel off the skins

COOKING WITH DRIED CHILLIES

In some markets, as many or more chillies are available in their dried form than are available fresh or powdered. Dried chillies can be turned into chilli powder or chilli purée.

To make chilli powder, lightly toast the chillies in the oven. Use an ungreased baking tray and set the oven at 200°C/400°F/Gas Mark 6. Toast them a few minutes, until they are somewhat brittle and give off a chilli fragrance. Do not allow them to darken – they will have a burned flavour that will ruin them. Let the toasted chillies cool. Remove the stems and seeds, cut or break them into pieces, and grind them in a food processor or spice grinder.

To make a purée, remove the stems and seeds and cut the chillies into two to four pieces. Put them in a deep, narrow heatproof bowl. Pour just enough boiling water over them to cover. Stir to be sure all pieces are covered. Let the chillies soak for 30 minutes. Pour the chillies and their soaking liquid into a blender or food processor. Purée until smooth. Strain to remove seeds and bits of skin, discard the solids. Use the strained sauce in cooking. The chillies also may be simmered in water, beer or beef or chicken stock, then puréed.

MEAT

Frontier-era chillies were made with beef "jerky", buffalo or venison. The vast majority of chillies today use beef or pork or a combination. One of chillie's charms is that the toughest, cheapest cuts of meat turn into tender morsels by the time a pot of chilli has simmered for an hour or so. Don't waste your money on tender steaks, chops or roasts. Chuck steak, topside, flank steak, pork shoulder and pork loin – all trimmed of excess fat – are good chilli cuts. Venison, now increasingly available in many supermarkets, has become a favourite again.

Ideally, your butcher sells a coarse grind of meat called chilli grind. It is coarser than hamburger, but finer than meat cut into small cubes. If you have a meat grinder, you can grind your own meat at home. An imperfect alternative is the food processor, which has an unfortunate tendency to produce an uneven mix of meat so finely ground that it has been turned to mush, and big chunks of meat that need to be chopped by hand. Throw a few 5-cm/2-in chunks of meat at a time into the food processor and use the pulse switch to grind the meat in very short bursts. Adding chunks of onion at the beginning helps. Otherwise, use hamburger or hand-cut the meat into 5–12-mm/¼–½-in dice.

FAT

Historically, chilli was cooked with a lot of fat – usually kidney suet, salt pork, lard or bacon dripping, all of which add more flavour than vegetable oil. And that is in addition to whatever fat was in the meat, which was sometimes a lot. Some say chilli eaters began crumbling savoury biscuits into their chilli because the crackers absorbed the grease that floated on top. Most of us have reduced the amount and type of fat we eat, and the most flavourful animal fats, like kidney suet, have fallen out of favour. Chilli can be made with a relatively small amount of fat – minimal amounts can be used to brown meat and onions. Most recipes in this cookbook call for vegetable oil, but equal amounts of other fats can be substituted.

BEANS

The International Chilli Society, based in the U.S., forbids the inclusion of beans in recipes entered in its cook-offs. But whether an ingredient in chilli or cooked separately and served on the side, beans are a natural mate for chilli. They provide a pleasant contrast in texture and flavour, and for the economical, help stretch a little meat a long way. Whenever possible, start with dried beans and soak and slow-cook them, especially when they are the primary ingredient in chilli. Canned beans tend to have a mushier texture, and a less distinct flavour.

HERBS AND SPICES

CORIANDER Coriander, also known as cilantro or Chinese parsley, is a pungent herb with a distinctive taste that its detractors call soapy. Ubiquitous in South Western dishes, it is not as common in chillies. It is best added in the last few minutes of cooking. Dried coriander lacks the flavour of fresh and is rarely used. Ground coriander seed is not a substitute for fresh coriander, but is sometimes added to chillies for its own flavour.

CUMIN Cumin is what gives chilli its distinctive flavour. This musky seasoning is usually used as a ground spice; however, chilli connisseurs toast the whole cumin seed in a small, dry frying pan, then grind it before adding to chilli. Toasting the seed enhances the flavour.

GARLIC Garlic, one of nature's greatest gifts to the cook, is one of the staples of a chilli-lover's larder. Chilli cooks often substitute garlic powder in competitions, where judges may deduct points for visible vegetables. If you are not entering your chilli in a cook-off, add lots of fresh garlic.

OREGANO With chilli powder and cumin, oregano is a basic chilli seasoning. Use dried, not ground, oregano. If toasting and grinding whole cumin seeds, add the oregano to the frying pan with the cumin for extra flavour.

◀ *Tortilla chips, sour cream, chopped onion, grated cheese and salsas are among the most popular chilli garnishes.*

GARNISHES

Some say it ruins perfectly good chilli, but many people say a bowl of chilli is incomplete without grated cheese sprinkled over the top. Others crumble handfuls of savoury biscuits into their chilli. But this is a more respectful debate than whether beans belong in chilli because, by definition, the garnishes are added by each individual to suit their taste, rather than imposed on them by a bullying cook.

In the U.S. grated Cheddar or Monterey jack cheese and chopped white or yellow onions are the most common garnishes. But without getting into the ridiculous, chilli is complemented by a large array of garnishes.

AVOCADOS Some people swear by them. I find their subtle flavour is overwhelmed by chilli. If you insist on topping your chilli with avocados, use the black-skinned Haas, which has more flavour than the smooth, green-skinned Fuerte.

CHEESE Grated Cheddar is the most popular. Feta and goat's cheeses, with their assertive flavours, are an unexpected treat with chilli.

CHILLIES Just in case your chilli doesn't have enough chilli flavour, garnish it with chopped or sliced fresh jalapeños. *Rajas*, strips of roasted (and sometimes fried) poblano chillies, are good. Hardcore chilliheads float tiny dried red hot chillies, such as chillipiquins, on top of their chilli, but this is more for looks than taste. The chillipiquins are rarely eaten, and care is taken that they are not broken and their fiery seeds spilled into the chilli.

CRISPS Crumbled corn or tortilla crisps add crunch and a salty flavour to chilli.

CORIANDER Sprinkle chopped fresh coriander over a bowl of chilli rather than cooking it in the chilli.

OLIVES Sliced black olives stand up surprisingly well to a spicy chilli.

ONIONS Bowls of chopped white or yellow onions are traditionally served with chilli, but red and spring onions are also good.

SAVOURY BISCUITS Crumbled over the top of chilli, these crackers add crunch and help sop up grease.

SOUR CREAM This adds a tangy flavour to chilli and takes the edge off fiery heat.

TORTILLAS Many chillis are delicious wrapped in warm corn or flour tortillas.

CHILLI FOR PURISTS

The original chillis of Texas and the American South West were little more than tough or dried meat boiled with chilli powders and other spices. Later, cooks added onion, garlic and tomato, but for some purists, even those ingredients were frowned on. For them, the addition of beans was sacrilege – although they often served beans on the side. For them, we offer the following 32 chilli recipes. They range from mild to smoke-coming-out-of-your-ears hot. Most use beef or pork, but some use venison, chicken or turkey. None of them includes beans.

Double Pork Ancho-Chipotle Chilli

225 g/8 oz pork sausagemeat

900 g/2 lb pork, cubed

2 tbsp vegetable oil

1½ medium onions, chopped

1 celery stick finely chopped

½ green pepper, finely chopped

3 garlic cloves, minced

250-ml/8 fl oz can tomato sauce

450 ml/¾ pt beef stock

4 ancho chillies

2 chipotle chillies, dried or canned

2 tbsp chilli powder

2 tsp ground cumin

2 tsp dried oregano

1 tsp celery salt

½ tsp sugar

1 tbsp lime juice

1–2 tsp salt

This chilli, made with cubed pork and pork sausage, has a thick, rich sauce. It is hot but not fiery. Big, meaty ancho chillies – dried poblanos – add a strong chilli taste that is not overpowered by the heat.

● Crumble the sausagemeat into a large frying pan and cook until a little fat is rendered. Add the cubed pork and cook until the meat is browned. Remove the meat and discard any fatty cooking juices. Heat the oil and sauté the onion, celery, green pepper and garlic for 5 minutes. Put the meat and vegetables in a large pan with the tomato sauce and beef stock. Bring to the boil, reduce heat and simmer.

● Cut the ancho chillies in half and remove the stems and seeds. If using dried chipotles, remove the stems. Put the dried chillies in a small, heatproof bowl and pour 250 ml/8 fl oz boiling water over them. Be sure all parts of the chillies are covered. Let the chillies stand in the hot water for 30 minutes. After soaking, put the chillies and their soaking water in a blender or food processor. If using canned chipotles, add them to the ancho chillies. Purée the chillies until a thick red sauce forms. Strain to remove seeds and bits of skin. Add the sauce to the chilli along with the remaining ingredients, except salt.

● When the meat has simmered for at least 1½ hours, add salt, taste and adjust seasonings.

Beef Chilli with Beer and Three Chillies

MAKES 4 SERVINGS

This is a traditional chilli of beef in a hot, velvety sauce of mild Anaheim chillies, hot New Mexico chillies and smoky chipotle chillies. Serve it with plain white rice to soak up the sauce.

● Split the dried chillies in half and remove the stems and seeds. (If using canned chipotles, do not add them at this point.) Put them in a small saucepan with the beer. Bring to the boil, reduce heat and simmer for 30 minutes, stirring occasionally to be sure all parts of the chillies are softening.

● While the chillies are cooking, heat 1 tablespoon of the oil in a frying pan or large saucepan and sauté the onions for 5 minutes, then add the garlic and sauté for 1 more minute. Remove the onions from the pan. Heat the remaining oil and cook the beef, stirring frequently, until the beef is lightly browned on all sides. Put the beef and onions in a pan with the beef stock. Boil, reduce heat and simmer.

● Put the chillies and cooking liquid in a blender or food processor. If using canned chipotle chillies, remove the stems and put the chipotles in the blender or food processor. Purée until a thick red sauce forms. Strain the sauce to remove the bits of skin, then add the sauce to the meat. Stir in the seasonings and sugar. Continue to simmer for at least 1 hour, until the meat is tender, adding beer, beef stock or water if needed. Add salt and adjust seasonings to taste.

ingredients

2 dried Anaheim chillies

2 dried New Mexico chillies

2 chipotle chillies, dried or canned

350 ml/12 fl oz beer

2 tbsp vegetable oil

1 medium onion, chopped

2 garlic cloves, minced

900 g/2 lb chuck steaks, trimmed and cubed

250ml/8 fl oz beef stock

1 tsp ground cumin

1 tsp paprika

1 tsp dried oregano

½ tsp sugar

about 1 tsp salt

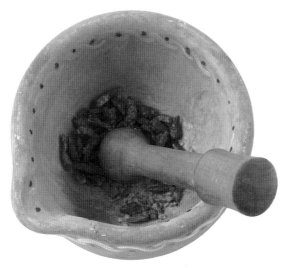

Rapid Fire Chilli

MAKES 4 TO 5 SERVINGS

ingredients

2 dried New Mexico chillies

2 dried Anaheim chillies

900 g/2 lb ground beef

1 tbsp vegetable oil

1 medium onion, chopped

250-ml/8-fl oz can tomato sauce

2 beef stock cubes

1 tsp garlic powder

1 tsp paprika

¼–½ tsp cayenne

1 tsp dried oregano

½ tsp ground coriander seed

½ tsp salt

● Cut the dried chillies in half and remove the stems and seeds. Put the chillies in a small, heatproof bowl and pour 250 ml/8 fl oz boiling water over them. Stir to be sure all parts of the chillies are covered with water. Let the chillies soak for 30 minutes. Put the chillies and soaking water in a blender or food processor and purée until a smooth sauce forms. Strain sauce.

● While the chillies are soaking, brown the beef in a large frying pan. Remove the beef with a slotted spoon. Drain and discard the fat. Heat the oil and sauté the onion for 5 minutes. Put the meat and onion in a large saucepan with the tomato sauce. Dissolve the stock cubes in 250 ml/8 fl oz boiling water and add to the meat.

● Bring to the boil, reduce heat and simmer for at least 20 minutes. Then add the chilli sauce and the remaining ingredients, except salt. Add a little water if needed while the chilli is cooking. Add salt, taste and adjust seasonings.

Boilermaker Chilli

MAKES 4 SERVINGS

ingredients

3 dried Anaheim chillies

2 dried New Mexico chillies

3 tbsp vegetable oil

900 g/2 lb cubed pork or beef

1 large onion, chopped

½ green pepper, chopped

1 celery stick, chopped

2 garlic cloves, minced

250 ml/8 fl oz tomato sauce

350 ml/12 fl oz beer

3 tbsp whisky

2 tsp ground cumin

1 tsp paprika

1 tsp dried oregano

½ tsp black pepper

about 1 tsp salt

● Split the dried chillies in half and remove the stems and seeds. Put the chillies in a small, heatproof bowl and pour 250 ml/8 fl oz boiling water over them. Soak the chillies for 30 minutes, stirring to make sure all parts of the chillies are covered with water.

● Heat 1 tablespoon of the oil in a frying pan and cook the meat, turning occasionally, until all sides are lightly browned. Remove the meat from the pan and set aside. Discard the fat in the pan. Heat the remaining oil and sauté the onion, green pepper, celery and garlic for 5 minutes. Put the meat and sautéed vegetables in a large pan with the tomato sauce, beer, 2 tablespoons of the whisky, and seasonings. Bring to the boil, reduce heat and simmer.

● Put the chillies and their soaking liquid in a blender or food processor. Purée until a smooth sauce forms. Strain to remove seeds and bits of skin and discard solids. Add the sauce to the chilli. Continue simmering the chilli, so the total simmering time is at least 1½ hours. Add salt and the remaining whisky. Taste and adjust seasonings.

▼ *Boilermaker Chilli*

Pork Chilli with Smoky Barbecue Sauce

MAKES 4 SERVINGS

*T*his chilli is only mildly spicy, but the pungent flavour is rounded out by the addition of smoky barbecue sauce.

ingredients

1 tbsp vegetable oil

900 g/2 lb pork, cubed

1½ onions, chopped

1 celery stick, finely chopped

750 ml/1¼ pt chicken stock

250-ml/8-fl oz can tomato sauce

1 tbsp smoky barbecue sauce

1 tbsp chilli powder

1 tsp dried oregano

about 1 tsp salt

● Heat the oil in a large, deep frying pan and cook the pork until lightly browned on all sides. Add the onion and celery and cook for 5 minutes.

● Add the remaining ingredients, except salt. Bring to the boil, reduce heat and simmer for 1½–2 hours, adding water if needed. Add salt to taste.

▶ *Pork Chilli with Smoky Barbecue Sauce*

Jon's Stout Stuff Chilli

MAKES 8 TO 10 SERVINGS

*J*on Engellenner is a connoisseur of beer. So much so that he brews his own. One of his hobbies is cooking with beer, and this chilli is a product of that. This is not a hot chilli, "just stout stuff," Jon says. In his words, this chilli "is complex, despite the simple recipe, and satisfying in small servings. Rather than searing its way through the taste buds, it melts across the palate like a hearty stew. It has the dense, chewable flavour of a patiently concocted gravy." Jon uses his own, home-brewed stout, but says any other will do.

ingredients

oil for frying

1.5 kg/3½ lb chuck steak, cut into cubes

450 g/1 lb ground chuck

2 large onions, diced

1 large green Anaheim chilli, diced

2 l/3½ pt stout

2 tsp hot chilli powder

2 tbsp salt

2 u 400-g/14-oz cans tomato sauce

2 u 400-g/14-oz cans tomatoes

1 tsp ground cumin

1 tsp paprika

2 tsp dried oregano

2–4 tbsp masa harina or flour

● In a big pan, heat a small amount of oil and brown the beef. Add the onions and green chilli and brown. Reduce the heat and add all the other ingredients, except the masa harina or flour. Cook at "high simmer" for 4 hours, stirring occasionally. Add the masa or flour dissolved in a little cold water to thicken.

Fiery Scotch Bonnet Chilli

Made with Scotch bonnet chillies, one of the hottest chillies on earth, this chilli is searingly hot. Serve it with rice to absorb the sauce. Equally hot habanero chillies can be substituted.

● Heat 1 tablespoon of the oil in a frying pan and brown the meat. Put the meat and beer in a large saucepan to simmer. Heat the remaining oil in the pan and sauté the chillies, onion, celery, green pepper and garlic for 5 minutes. Add to the meat the remaining ingredients, except the masa harina and salt.

● Bring to the boil, reduce heat, cover and simmer for at least 1 hour, adding water or beer if necessary. Mix the masa harina or cornmeal with a little warm water to make a smooth paste and add it to the chilli to thicken. Add salt to taste.

ingredients

3 tbsp vegetable oil

900 g/2 lb beef or pork, cubed

350 ml/12 fl oz beer

2 Scotch bonnet chillies, unseeded, minced

1 large onion, chopped

1 celery stick, minced

½ green pepper, chopped

2 garlic cloves, minced

1 tsp ground coriander

1 tsp paprika

1 tsp ground cumin

1 tsp sugar

1 tbsp fresh lime juice

1 tbsp masa harina or cornmeal

about 1 tsp salt

Hair-on-your-chest Chilli

Here is a chilli that will test the asbestos palate and stomach of chilli-lovers who boast about how hot they like their chilli. It is made with habanero chillies, the hottest chillies on earth. The only substitute is the equally incendiary Scotch bonnet chilli. This chilli also uses chipotle chillies – smoked jalapeños – but just for the smoky flavour, since the jalapeño is mild in comparison to the habanero. It's finished off with a shot of tequila.

● Crumble the sausagemeat into a frying pan and fry until a little fat runs. Add the cubed pork and cook until the meat has browned. Put the meat in a large pan with the beer and beef stock. Bring to the boil, reduce heat and simmer. Discard any fat from the pan. Heat the oil in the frying pan and sauté the onion for 5 minutes. Add the onion to the pork.

● Roast the Anaheim chillies under the grill until the skin has blackened and blistered on all sides. Put the chillies in a paper bag, covered heatproof bowl, or foil pouch, and seal. After the chillies have steamed in the bag, bowl, or foil for 10 minutes, remove them. Peel the chillies and remove the stems and seeds. Put the Anaheim chillies in a blender or

ingredients

225 g/8 oz pork sausagemeat

900 g/2 lb pork, cubed

350 ml/12 fl oz beer

450 ml/¾ pt beef stock

1 tbsp vegetable oil

1½ medium onions, chopped

3 Anaheim chillies

2 canned chipotle chillies

2 habanero chillies, unseeded, minced

2 tbsp chilli powder

2 tsp ground cumin

1 tsp each dried oregano, ground coriander seed and black pepper

1 tbsp masa harina

about 1 tsp salt

3 tbsp tequila

food processor. Remove the stems from the chipotles, and add them to the Anaheims. To add volume, add a little bit of the chilli cooking liquid. Purée until smooth. If you don't want to chop the habaneros by hand, add them to the blender after the mixture is puréed. Blend or process in just a few short bursts – the habaneros should be chopped but not puréed. Add the chilli mixture to the stew.

● Add the chilli powder, cumin, oregano, coriander and black pepper. Let the chilli continue simmering – the meat should cook for a minimum of 1½ hours. When the chilli is well cooked, mix the masa harina with 2 tablespoons cold water to make a paste, then add the paste to the chilli. Add salt, taste and adjust seasonings. Add the tequila and serve.

▶ *Hair-on-your-chest Chilli*

Teary-eyed Beef and Pork Chilli

MAKES 4 SERVINGS

*T*his hot chilli gets its heat from pure ground chilli de arbol powder. This is a purist's chilli – nothing but meat, onion and sauce that is full of flavour.

ingredients

3 tbsp vegetable oil

450 g/1 lb beef, cubed

450 g/1 lb pork, cubed

350 ml/12 fl oz beef stock

1½ onions, chopped

250-ml/8-fl oz can tomato sauce

1 tsp celery salt

1 tsp garlic powder

2 tbsp chilli powder

1 tsp pure chilli de arbol powder

2 tsp ground cumin

1 tsp dried marjoram

½ tsp sugar

1 tbsp masa harina

1–2 tsp salt

● Heat 1 tablespoon of the oil in a large frying pan and cook the beef and pork until browned. Remove the meat with a slotted spoon and put it in a large saucepan with the beef stock. Bring to the boil, reduce heat and simmer. Discard greasy cooking liquids from the frying pan.

● Heat the remaining oil in the frying pan and sauté the onion for 5 minutes. Add the onion to the meat with the remaining ingredients, except the masa harina and salt. Simmer the chilli for at least 1 hour. Mix the masa harina with 2 tablespoons water to form a paste. Add the paste to the chilli and stir well. Add salt, taste and adjust seasonings.

Three Flames Beef Chilli

MAKES 4 SERVINGS

*T*his is a very hot chilli, but toasting the cumin and oregano enhances their flavours so they are not drowned out by the heat of three pure chilli powders – the hot chilli de arbol and cayenne and the milder pasilla.

● Cook the bacon in a frying pan. When done, set it on paper towels to drain and cool. You will need about 3 tablespoons of dripping – discard any excess.

● Reheat 1 tablespoon of the dripping and cook the beef until browned. Remove the beef. Add up to 2 tablespoons dripping and heat. Add the onion, green pepper, and garlic, and sauté for 5 minutes. Put the beef and sautéed vegetables in a large saucepan. Add the beer, tomato sauce and chilli powders. Bring to the boil, reduce heat and simmer.

● Heat a small frying pan and add the cumin seeds and oregano. Cook, gently shaking the pan occasionally so they do not scorch, until they are brown. Remove and grind in a pestle and mortar, a small grinder, or place them between two sheets of wax paper and crush with the edge of a rolling pin. Add to the chilli with the sugar.

● Simmer the meat for at least 1½ hours. Just before serving, crumble the bacon and add. Add the salt, taste and adjust seasonings.

ingredients

4 rashers of bacon

900 g/2 lb beef, cubed

1½ medium onions, chopped

½ green pepper, finely chopped

4 garlic cloves, minced

350 ml/12 fl oz beer

250-ml/8-fl oz tomato sauce

1 tbsp pure chilli de arbol powder

2 tbsp pure pasilla chilli powder

½ tsp cayenne

2 tsp whole cumin seeds

2 tsp dried oregano

½ tsp sugar

about 1 tsp salt

Terry's Chilli for the Tender Palate

ingredients

3 tbsp vegetable oil

900 g/2 lb beef, cubed

1 medium onion, chopped

4 garlic cloves, minced

450 ml/¾ pt beef stock

250-ml/8-fl oz can tomato sauce

3 tbsp chilli powder

2 tsp dried oregano

about 1 tsp salt

My husband grew up in Baltimore. By the time he moved to Austin, Texas, Terry was an adult who had never developed a taste for spicy food. He left Texas less than three years later with a story about a woman and debts, but I believe the truth is that he was run out one night when he made the mistake of telling a Texan he didn't like chilli. Here is a mild chilli I make just for him. It is delicious over steamed white rice.

● Heat 1 tablespoon of the oil in a frying pan and cook the beef until browned on all sides. With a slotted spoon, remove the beef to a large saucepan. Discard the fatty cooking liquids. Heat the remaining oil in the frying pan and sauté the onion and garlic for 5 minutes. Add the onion and garlic to the beef. Add the remaining ingredients, except salt.

● Bring to the boil, reduce heat and simmer for at least 1½ hours, adding water or beef stock if needed. Add salt, taste and adjust seasonings.

New Mexico Chilli with Lamb

ingredients

2 tbsp vegetable oil

900 g/2 lb lamb, cubed

1½ medium onions, chopped

4 garlic cloves, minced

8 New Mexico, Anaheim, or poblano chillies or a combination

250-ml/8-fl oz can tomato sauce

2–4 jalapeño or serrano chillies, unseeded, minced

1 tsp dried oregano

¼ tsp dried sage

25 g/1 oz chopped fresh coriander

about 1 tsp salt

Lamb is a staple of the Navajo Indians of New Mexico and is frequently prepared in stews. Here it is paired with green chillies. Fresh New Mexico green chillies are traditional, but Anaheim or poblano chillies or a combination can be substituted. The jalapeño or serrano chillies add the heat. The strong flavour of lamb overwhelms a mild chilli and is best in a very spicy-hot stew. Serve with Navajo fried bread or plain steamed rice.

● In a large, deep frying pan, heat the oil and cook the lamb until browned on all sides. If the pan is large enough, add the onion and garlic and cook for 5 minutes longer, then transfer to a large saucepan. If the pan is not large enough, remove the lamb to a large saucepan. Add more oil to the pan, if needed. Sauté the onion and garlic for 5 minutes, then add to the lamb. Add about 250 ml/8 fl oz water. Bring to the boil, reduce heat and simmer for at least 1½ hours. Add water if needed.

● While the lamb is simmering, roast the green chillies (but not the jalapeños or serranos). Place them under the grill and cook, turning, until all sides are blistered and blackened. Remove the chillies and immediately put them in a paper bag or covered bowl to steam for at least 10 minutes. Peel the chillies and remove the stems and seeds.

● Chop half the chillies and add them to the stew. Put the other half in a blender or food processor with the tomato sauce and purée until smooth. Add the purée to the stew, along with the jalapeños or serranos, the oregano and sage. About 10 minutes before the chilli is done, add the fresh coriander and salt. Taste and adjust seasonings.

▼ *New Mexico Chilli with Lamb*

Beef and Sausage Chilli

225 g/8 oz Italian-style pork sausage

900 g/2 lb beef, cubed

1 medium onion, chopped

1 green pepper, chopped

2 garlic cloves, minced

450 ml/¾ pt beef stock

250-ml/8-fl oz can tomato sauce

2 tbsp chilli powder

2 tsp ground cumin

about 1 tsp Tabasco or other hot pepper sauce

about 1 tsp salt

The seasonings in the Italian sausage add an extra dimension of flavour to this basic moderate chilli. To adjust the heat, increase or decrease the amount of Tabasco sauce.

● Crumble the sausage into a large, deep frying pan and cook for about 2 minutes, until some of the fat has run. Add the beef and cook, turning occasionally, until the meat is lightly browned. Spoon off the excess fat. Add the onion, green pepper and garlic and cook for 5 minutes.

● Transfer the mixture to a large saucepan. Add the remaining ingredients, except salt. Bring to the boil, reduce heat and simmer until the meat is tender, about 1½ hours. Add water as needed. Add salt, taste and adjust seasonings.

Jalapeño Chilli

2 tbsp vegetable oil

900 g/2 lb beef or pork, cubed

1 medium onion, chopped

6 jalapeño chillies, unseeded, minced

2 garlic cloves, minced

450 ml/¾ pt beef stock

250-ml/8-fl oz can tomato sauce

2 tbsp chilli powder

1 tsp ground cumin

1 tsp dried oregano

about 1 tsp salt

This is a hot but simple chilli, seasoned with chilli powder and unseeded fresh jalapeños. To reduce the heat, remove the seeds and veins from the jalapeños.

● Heat 1 tablespoon of the oil in a frying pan and cook the meat until browned. Remove the meat with a slotted spoon. Discard the greasy cooking liquids. Heat the remaining oil and sauté the onion, jalapeños and garlic for 5 minutes.

● Put the meat, vegetables, beef stock and 250 ml/8 fl oz water in a large saucepan. Stir in the tomato sauce, chilli powder, cumin and oregano. Bring to the boil, reduce heat and simmer for at least 1½ hours until the meat is tender. Stir occasionally and add water if needed. Add salt, taste and adjust seasonings.

Scorcher Chilli

This chilli is for Texas purists – those who want no beans and no tomatoes in a scorchingly hot but simple chilli. The beer-based sauce gets its heat from pure chilli de arbol powder and unseeded jalapeños, while pasilla and mild New Mexico or California pure chilli powders fill out the chilli flavour.

● Heat 1 tablespoon of the oil in a frying pan and cook the beef until browned. With a slotted spoon, remove the meat. Discard the greasy cooking liquids. Heat the remaining oil in the pan and sauté the onion for 5 minutes. Put the beef, onion and beer in a large saucepan. While the mixture is heating, dissolve the stock cubes in 250 ml/8 fl oz hot water. Add the stock plus 450 ml/¾ pt water to the meat. Bring to the boil. Add the remaining ingredients, except the masa harina and salt. Simmer until the meat is tender, at least 1½ hours, adding water if needed.

● Mix the masa harina with 3 tablespoons water and stir to make a paste. Add to the chilli and cook for 2 minutes. Add salt, taste and adjust seasonings.

ingredients

2 tbsp vegetable oil

900 g/2 lb beef, cubed

1 onion, chopped

350 ml/12 fl oz beer

2 beef stock cubes

3 jalapeño chillies, unseeded, minced

1 tbsp pure pasilla chilli powder

1 tbsp mild New Mexico or California chilli powder

1 tsp chilli de arbol powder

2 tsp ground cumin

2 tsp ground oregano

1 tsp garlic powder

1 tsp ground coriander

2 tbsp masa harina

about ½ tsp salt

◀ *Scorcher Chilli*

Simple Beef and Salsa Chilli

MAKES 4 SERVINGS

*T*his is a very easy-to-make chilli, with bottled salsa providing the heart of the sauce. The spiciness will depend on the type of salsa you use, but can be increased by adding cayenne. The salsa and stock cubes may provide enough salt.

ingredients

2 tbsp vegetable oil

900 g/2 lb beef, cubed

1 medium onion, chopped

450 ml/¾ pt bottled red salsa, preferably chunky

250-ml/8-fl oz can tomato sauce

2 beef stock cubes

3 tbsp chilli powder

1 tsp ground cumin

1 tsp dried oregano

cayenne to taste

salt, if needed

● Heat 1 tablespoon of the oil in a frying pan and cook the beef until lightly browned. Remove the meat with a slotted spoon. Discard the greasy cooking liquids. Heat the remaining oil in the pan and sauté the onion for 5 minutes.

● Put the beef, onion, salsa and tomato sauce into a large saucepan. Dissolve the stock cubes in 450 ml/¾ pt hot water and add to the chilli. Add the chilli powder, cumin and oregano. Bring to the boil, reduce heat and simmer until the meat is tender, about 1½ hours. Stir occasionally, adding water if needed. If desired, add cayenne and salt to taste.

Chilli Verde Stew

MAKES 4 TO 6 SERVINGS

Although I grew up in Southern California where spices are added with a heavy hand, for many years my experience with fresh chillies was fairly limited. One day I was experimenting with a recipe for green chilli stew. It called for poblano chillies, described as green and triangular. My local greengrocer had a large selection of fresh chillies, but a single sign that said only "red and green chillies". The sales person pointed out the poblanos. To me, they looked like jalapeños, but they were green and somewhat triangular, so I bought a dozen. I roasted and peeled them, and added them to the stew, seeds and all. Then I sampled it. I thought the skin was going to wither right off my tongue! It was the hottest food I'd ever put in my mouth. At dinner, none of us could stand the scorchingly hot stew, so we just ate cornbread, chilli con queso and tortilla chips. Of course the chillies were jalapeños – a few days later, a friend introduced me to poblanos, which look nothing like jalapeños. Made with poblanos, the stew is pleasantly spicy.

- Roast the chillies under the grill, turning often with tongs, until they are almost totally black, about 10 minutes. Put the chillies in a plastic or paper bag, close the bag and let them sit for 20 minutes. Remove them one by one, stem and seed them and cut into strips.
- Dredge the meat in the flour. Heat 1 tablespoon of the margarine in a large frying pan and brown the meat. Put the meat in a large saucepan. Heat the remaining margarine and sauté the onions and garlic. Add them, with the remaining ingredients, to the stew. Add 450 ml/¾ pt of water. Simmer the stew over low heat for 1 hour.

ingredients

10–12 poblano chillies

900 g/2 lb pork shoulder, cubed

25 g/1 oz plain flour

25 g/1 oz margarine

2 large onions, chopped

4 garlic cloves, minced

450 g/1 lb whole canned tomatoes, coarsely chopped

250-ml/8-fl oz can tomato sauce

1 tsp salt

pinch black pepper

Eye-popping Chilli with Corn

MAKES 4 TO 6 SERVINGS

ingredients

3 tbsp vegetable oil

350 ml/12 fl oz bottled hot salsa

2 beef stock cubes

1 medium onion, chopped

900 g/2 lb beef, cubed or coarsely ground

2 tbsp hot New Mexico chilli powder

2 tbsp chilli powder

1 tsp ground cumin

1 tsp dried oregano

1 tsp garlic powder

1 tsp celery salt

250 g/9 oz corn

about 1 tsp salt

*T*his chilli starts with a bottled hot salsa and gets hotter with New Mexico chilli powder. The corn adds a pleasing sweetness and a bit of crunch. If you have fresh corn, hold it over the pan as you cut the corn off the cob so that the milky liquid drips into the chilli. Otherwise, frozen corn is fine.

● Heat 1 tablespoon of the oil in a large saucepan. When the oil is sizzling hot, add the salsa and fry for 5 minutes. Dissolve the stock cubes in 250 ml/ 8 fl oz boiling water and add it to the salsa, with 450 ml/¾ pt more water.

● Heat 1 tablespoon of the oil in a frying pan and sauté the onion for 5 minutes. Add the onion to the salsa. Heat the remaining oil and cook the beef until lightly browned. Add to the salsa with the remaining ingredients, except the corn and salt. Simmer for 1 hour. Add the corn and simmer for 30 minutes. Add salt, taste and adjust seasonings.

Savoury Beef Chilli

Small amounts of unsweetened cocoa and cinnamon are the secret ingredients in this tasty chilli. Your kitchen may smell like cappuccino, but the ingredients will remain a mystery in the chilli. Cocoa deepens the flavour of the sauce, giving it rich undertones.

● Heat 1 tablespoon of the oil in a frying pan and cook the beef until browned. Remove the meat with a slotted spoon and discard the greasy cooking liquids. Heat the remaining oil in the pan and sauté the onion, celery, green pepper and garlic for 5 minutes.

● Put the beef and vegetables in a large saucepan with the beer, tomato sauce and 450 ml/¾ pt water. Add jalapeños, bay leaves, chilli powder, cocoa and cinnamon. Bring to the boil, reduce heat and simmer until the pork is tender, at least 1½ hours. Stir occasionally and add water if needed.

● Add the lime juice and Tabasco sauce and cook for 5 minutes. Add salt, taste and adjust seasonings.

ingredients

3 tbsp vegetable oil

900 g/2 lb beef, cubed

1½ onions, chopped

1 celery stick, finely chopped

½ green pepper, finely chopped

2 garlic cloves, minced

350-ml/12-fl oz bottle beer

250-ml/8-fl oz can tomato sauce

2 jalapeño chillies, unseeded, minced

2 bay leaves

3 tbsp chilli powder

2 tsp unsweetened cocoa

⅛ tsp ground cinnamon

1 tbsp lime juice

at least ½ tsp Tabasco or other hot pepper sauce

1–2 tsp salt

Pork and Chorizo Chilli

ingredients

6 large dried chillies, such as New Mexico, California, anchos, or a combination

3 tbsp vegetable oil

900 g/2 lb pork, cubed

1½ medium onions, chopped

1 celery stick, finely chopped

⅓ green pepper, chopped

4 garlic cloves, minced

2 beef stock cubes

2 tsp ground cumin

2 tsp dried oregano

1 tsp ground coriander

¼ tsp dried sage

½ tsp sugar

225 g/8 oz chorizo sausage (unsmoked)

2 tbsp masa harina

1–2 tsp salt

This is a very hearty chilli with bold flavours. Made with a combination of two dried California chillies, two dried New Mexico chillies, and two dried chillies negros, it is hot but not fiery. Vary the chillies to suit your taste.

● Remove the stems and seeds from the dried chillies. Cut each chilli in several pieces, place in a small heatproof bowl and add 250 ml/8 fl oz boiling water. Stir to be sure all pieces of chillies are covered. Let soak for 30 minutes.

● Meanwhile, heat 1 tablespoon of the oil in a frying pan and cook the pork, stirring occasionally, until lightly browned. Remove the meat with a slotted spoon and discard the greasy cooking liquids. Heat the remaining oil in the pan and sauté the onion, celery, green pepper and garlic for 5 minutes.

● Put the pork and vegetables in a large saucepan and add water to cover. Bring to the boil, reduce heat and simmer. Dissolve the stock cubes in 250 ml/8 fl oz hot water and add to the chilli. Add the cumin, oregano, coriander, sage and sugar.

● Put the dried chillies and their soaking liquid in a blender or food processor. Purée until smooth. Strain to remove seeds and bits of skin and discard solids. Add the sauce to the chilli.

● After the chilli has cooked about 1 hour, crumble the chorizo into a hot frying pan and fry for 7–8 minutes, until all the fat has run. Remove from the heat and tilt the pan to drain the fat. With a slotted spoon, remove the chorizo and add to the chilli. Discard the fat.

● Continue simmering until the pork is tender, at least 1½ hours, adding water if needed. When the chilli is ready, dissolve the masa harina in 4 table-spoons cold water to make a paste. Add to the chilli and stir well. Add salt, taste and adjust seasonings.

California Chilli Buffet

This buffet starts with a spicy Texas-style chilli with ground beef, cubed beef, cubed pork and pork sausage, but it becomes a California-style meal with such trimmings as black olives, Avocado Salsa and goat's cheese. Serve the chilli next to a big pot of black beans, and let guests add their own toppings.

ingredients

BUFFET:

Chilli, Smoky Black Beans (page 110) or Hot Black Beans (page 110), grated Cheddar cheese, crumbled goat's cheese, sliced black olives, Avocado Salsa (page 122), chopped onions, chopped fresh coriander, chopped jalapeño chillies, and sour cream.

CHILLI:

4–6 tbsp vegetable oil

900 g/2 lb beef, cubed

900 g/2 lb pork, cubed

900 g/2 lb ground beef

450 g/1 lb pork sausage

2 large onions, chopped

8 garlic cloves, minced

1.5 l/2½ pt beef stock

450 ml/¾ pt can tomato purée

4 tsp whole cumin seed

1 tbsp dried oregano

1 tsp dried basil

1 tsp celery seed

1 tsp coriander seed

50 g/2 oz chilli powder

3 tbsp hot New Mexico chilli powder

juice of 1 lime

1 tsp sugar

1–3 tsp salt

● You will need to cook the meat in batches. Unless you have a really large frying pan, don't cook more than 625 g/1½ lb at a time. You can mix the cubed beef and pork or the ground beef and sausage, but don't try to cook ground meat with cubed meat. The ground meat does not need to be cooked in oil. Heat about 1 tablespoon oil for each batch of cubed meat. Put the cooked meat in a large stockpot, but don't put it over the heat until you add liquid.

● After cooking the meats, heat 2 tablespoons oil in the frying pan and sauté the onion and garlic for 5 minutes. Add the onion to the stockpot with the meat. Add the beef stock and tomato purée and stir well. Bring to the boil, then reduce heat and simmer for about 1½ hours. Stir occasionally and add water if needed.

● In a small, dry frying pan, add the cumin seed, oregano, basil, celery seed and coriander seed. Toast over medium heat, shaking the pan frequently so the seeds don't scorch. Cook until the seeds are fragrant and lightly toasted, but take care that they do not burn. Remove from the heat and let seeds cool for 5–10 minutes. Grind them in a nut grinder, pestle and mortar, or crush them with the edge of a rolling pin. Add to the chilli. Add the chilli powders, mix well, and let the stew continue simmering.

● About 30 minutes before the chilli is done, add the lime juice and sugar, and continue simmering. When the meat is very tender, add salt, taste and adjust seasonings.

Donna Roberts' Hearty Venison Chilli

MAKES 4 TO 6 SERVINGS

ingredients

900 g/2 lb ground venison

2 medium onions, chopped

4 garlic cloves, minced

450-ml/¾ pt can tomato sauce

4 tbsp chilli powder

1 tsp ground cumin

½ tsp cayenne

2 tsp Worcestershire sauce

1½ tsp salt

5 whole cloves

2 tsp allspice

My husband, who loves to write about cars as much as I love to write about food, was interviewing Ross Roberts, vice president and general manager of Ford Motor Company, when he mentioned that I was working on a chilli cookbook. Roberts, a Texan who loves chilli, sent me this recipe for his wife's chilli. The cloves and allspice complement the venison, while the chilli powder and cayenne make a pleasantly spicy chilli.

● Cover the meat with water and cook in a large saucepan, stirring until the meat crumbles. Stir in all the remaining ingredients. Cook for 30 minutes at medium heat. Simmer, covered, for 2 hours. Keep checking until the chilli is the desired consistency.

Turkey Chilli

MAKES 6 SERVINGS

ingredients

2 dried chillies negros

2 dried Anaheim (California) chillies

2–3 tbsp vegetable oil

175 g/6 oz turkey sausage

450 g/1 lb ground turkey

1 medium onion, chopped

1 celery stick, chopped

450 ml/¾ pt chicken stock

250-ml/8-fl oz tomato sauce

1 tsp ground cumin

1 tsp dried oregano

¼ tsp cayenne or to taste

425-g/15-oz can frijoles colorados, drained (small red beans)

about 1 tsp salt

This is a very hearty chilli with bold flavours. It is moderately hot, made with dried Anaheim chillies, chillies negros and a little cayenne, but other large dried chillies can be substituted. Ground turkey and turkey sausage provide a lower-fat alternative to beef and pork, but check the packaging to be sure ground turkey and turkey sausage contain 10 per cent fat or less. Some turkey products contain a lot of turkey fat and skin, giving them a higher fat content than ground pork or beef.

● Remove the stems and seeds from the chillies, then cut each chilli in several pieces. Put the pieces in a small heatproof bowl and add 250 ml/8 fl oz boiling water. Stir to be sure all the pieces of chilli are covered by water. Let soak for 30 minutes.

● Meanwhile, put about 1 teaspoon oil in a large frying pan and crumble in the turkey sausage. If, after 2–3 minutes, the sausage doesn't render any additional fat, add about 2 teaspoons more oil to the pan. Crumble the ground turkey into the pan. Cook until the meat is lightly browned. Remove from the pan.

● Heat 1½ tablespoons oil in the pan and

▲ Turkey Chilli

sauté the onion and celery for 5 minutes.
Put the meat and vegetables in a large
saucepan and add the chicken stock,
tomato sauce and spices. Bring to the
boil, reduce heat and simmer.

● Put the chillies and soaking liquid in a
blender or food processor and purée until
smooth. Strain to remove seeds and bits
of skin, and discard solids. Add the sauce
to the chilli.

● Simmer the chilli for at least 1 hour,
adding water or chicken stock if needed.
Add the beans and cook for 5 minutes.
Add salt, taste and adjust seasonings.

Beef and Chorizo Chilli

Chorizo, a Spanish pork sausage, gives this chilli a richer flavour. It is a moderately hot, robust chilli that uses regular chilli powder and "hot" or "Mexican" chilli powder, but no cumin other than that in the two chilli powder blends. Fresh coriander and spring onion added at the end provide a nice contrast in flavour and texture.

ingredients

3 tbsp vegetable oil

900 g/2 lb beef, cubed

1½ medium onions, chopped

1 celery stick, finely chopped

3 garlic cloves, minced

2 beef stock cubes

250-ml/8-fl oz can tomato sauce

2 tbsp chilli powder

2 tbsp "hot" or "Mexican" chilli powder

1 tsp dried oregano

350 g/12 oz chorizo sausage (unsmoked)

about 1 tsp salt

15 g/½ oz fresh coriander, chopped

⅓ cup spring onions, chopped

● Heat 1 tablespoon of the oil in a frying pan and cook the beef until brown. Remove the meat with a slotted spoon and set aside. Discard the greasy cooking liquid. Heat the remaining oil in the pan and sauté the onion, celery, and garlic for 5 minutes. Put the cooked beef and vegetables in a large saucepan and barely cover with water. Bring to the boil, reduce heat and simmer. Dissolve the stock cubes in 250 ml/8 fl oz hot water, and add to the chilli. Add the tomato sauce, chilli powders and oregano to the chilli. Stir the chilli, adding water if needed.

● After the chilli has cooked for about 1 hour, crumble the chorizo into a frying pan and cook over medium heat for 7–8 minutes, until all the fat has run. Remove the pan from the heat and tilt to drain the fat. Remove the sausage with a slotted spoon and add to the chilli. Discard the fat.

● Continue simmering the chilli until the beef is tender, a total of at least 1½ hours. Just before serving, add salt, taste and adjust seasonings. Stir in the coriander and spring onions.

Walt and Carolyn's Texas Bowl of Red

MAKES 6 SERVINGS

ingredients

1.4 kg/3 lb brisket

50–75 g/2–3 oz kidney suet

3 heaped tbsp chilli powder

1 tbsp dried oregano

1 tbsp ground cumin

1 tbsp cayenne

1 tbsp salt

1 tbsp Tabasco sauce

4–8 garlic cloves, minced

I grew up thinking of chilli as a mild mixture of ground beef and kidney beans. Walt Wiley, a transplanted Texan and my co-worker on a California newspaper, was the first to tell me the Texas side of the chilli story. True chilli has no beans, no tomatoes, no onions, and is never mild. His wife, Carolyn, a gourmet cook, adapted this recipe from one in Frank X. Tolbert's classic "A Bowl of Red". They suggest serving it over a mound of Fritos to make Frito Pie, a teenage favourite. "We found that chilli made like this was a lot like the chilli we remembered from our childhoods in North Texas," Walt said. "You could get a bowl for a quarter at the bus station or any greasy spoon café."

● Trim the fat off the brisket and cut the brisket into cubes about the size of the end of your thumb. Chop up and render the kidney suet and brown the brisket in that. Put the meat and fat in a pan with enough water to cover the meat by about 2.5 cm/1 in. Add the chilli powder. Bring to the boil, reduce heat and simmer for 30 minutes. Add oregano, cumin, cayenne, salt, Tabasco and garlic.

● Let the chilli simmer for another 45 minutes or so. Don't stir it too much and don't let it boil dry and scorch, but don't add so much water that it is soupy. There will be a lot of grease, which probably should be skimmed.

Texas Waterfront Chipotle Pork Chilli

MAKES 4 SERVINGS

This chilli is made with Anaheim and chipotle chillies, but it will be the chipotles that will make you want to throw yourself in the river to cool off. This is a true Texas chilli, made with no beans and no tomatoes, thickened with cracker crumbs.

ingredients

3 tbsp vegetable oil

1½ medium onions, chopped

3 garlic cloves, minced

900 g/2 lb pork, diced

450 ml/¾ pt chicken stock

4 Anaheim chillies

4 canned chipotle chillies

1 tbsp chilli powder

1 tsp ground cumin

2 tsp dried oregano

about 2 tbsp cracker crumbs

about ½ tsp salt

● Heat 2 tablespoons of the oil in a large frying pan and sauté the onion and garlic for 5 minutes. Remove the onion to a large saucepan and set aside. Heat the remaining oil and cook the pork until lightly browned on all sides. Add the pork to the saucepan, then the chicken stock. Bring to the boil, stirring well, then reduce heat and simmer, adding water if needed.

● Roast the Anaheim chillies under the grill, turning until the skin on all sides is blistered and mostly blackened. Remove from the grill and put in a paper bag, a foil envelope, or a small covered bowl. Let steam for at least 10 minutes. Peel off the skin and remove the seeds. Cut each chilli across its width into several pieces. Put the Anaheims in a blender or food processor. Remove the stems from the chipotles, add them to the Anaheims and purée. Add the purée to the chilli. Add the remaining ingredients, except the cracker crumbs and salt.

● When the meat has simmered for 1½ hours, add the cracker crumbs to thicken. Taste, add salt if needed and adjust seasonings.

Pork Chilli with Corn and Jalapeños

*T*his is a moderately hot chilli if you don't remove the seeds and veins from the jalapeños, a pleasantly spicy chilli if you remove them. It is thick with vegetables, including corn, which adds a slight sweetness. Use frozen corn or fresh, cut straight from the cob into the pan.

ingredients

3 tbsp vegetable oil

900 g/2 lb pork, diced

450 g/1 lb pork sausage

1½ medium onions, chopped

1 celery stick, finely chopped

½ green pepper, finely chopped

3 garlic cloves, minced

2 beef stock cubes

3 tbsp chilli powder

1 tbsp ancho chilli powder

1 tsp ground cumin

1 tsp dried oregano

corn (about 2 ears)

2 jalapeño chillies, minced

2 tbsp fresh coriander, chopped

about 1 tsp salt

● Heat 1 tablespoon of the oil in a large frying pan and cook the pork until lightly browned. Put the pork in a saucepan, but do not put it on the heat yet. Crumble the sausage into the frying pan and cook until browned. Drain off and discard any grease. Add the sausage to the pork. Heat the remaining oil in the frying pan and sauté the onions, celery, green pepper and garlic for 5 minutes and add to the pork.

● Dissolve the stock cubes in 250 ml/ 8 fl oz boiling water. Add to the pork with 450 ml/¾ pt water. Add the spices to the pork, stir well. Bring to the boil, reduce heat and simmer until the pork is very tender, about 1½ hours.

● About 30 minutes before the chilli is done, add the corn and jalapeños. About 5 minutes before it is done, add the coriander. Add salt, taste, and adjust seasonings.

Bloody Mary Chilli

*T*his is a moderately spicy chilli seasoned with three pure chilli powders and thickened with cracker crumbs.

ingredients

2 tbsp vegetable oil

1 medium onion, chopped

900 g/2 lb beef, diced

450 ml/¾ pt beef stock

350 ml/12 fl oz tomato juice or Bloody Mary mix

1 tbsp mild New Mexico chilli powder

1 tbsp hot chilli powder

1 tbsp ancho chilli powder

2 tsp ground cumin

2 tsp dried oregano

1 tsp garlic powder

about 2 tbsp cracker crumbs

● Heat 1 tablespoon of the oil in a frying pan and sauté the onion for 5 minutes. Remove the onion. Add the remaining oil and heat. Cook the beef until lightly browned.

● Put the onion, beef and remaining ingredients, except the crumbs and salt,

in a large saucepan. Stir well. Bring to the boil, reduce heat and simmer for 1½ hours. Stir occasionally and add water if needed. Add the cracker crumbs to thicken. Add ½–1 teaspoon of salt, taste and adjust seasonings.

▶ *Bloody Mary Chilli*

Ground Beef and Turkey Chilli with Three Chilli Powders

MAKES 4 SERVINGS

ingredients

1 tbsp vegetable oil

1 onion, chopped

4 garlic cloves, minced

450 g/1 lb ground beef

450 g/1 lb ground turkey

450 ml/¾ pt beef or chicken stock

250-ml/8-fl oz can tomato sauce

1 tbsp California chilli powder

1 tbsp ancho chilli powder

1 tbsp hot New Mexico chilli powder

1 tsp ground cumin

1 tsp dried oregano

1 tsp dried basil

1 tsp celery salt

The combination of California, ancho and New Mexico chilli powders provides a rich range of chilli flavours. This is pleasantly spicy, and can be made hotter by adding New Mexico chilli powder.

● Heat the oil in a frying pan and sauté the onion and garlic for 5 minutes. Put the vegetables in a large saucepan and set aside. Brown the beef, then the turkey in the frying pan, adding each to the saucepan. Add the stock, 450 ml/¾ pt water, tomato sauce and seasonings to the saucepan. Bring to the boil, stirring well. Reduce the heat and simmer for 1–1½ hours, stirring occasionally and adding water if needed. Taste, adjust seasonings and add salt if desired.

Cuisinart Chilli

MAKES 4 SERVINGS

ingredients

1 large onion, chopped

3 garlic cloves, minced

3 jalapeño chillies

900 g/2 lb chuck steak or other inexpensive cut of beef

3 tbsp vegetable oil

450 ml/¾ pt beef stock

250-ml/8-fl oz can tomato sauce

3 tbsp chilli powder

1 tsp ground cumin

1 tsp dried oregano

½ tsp dried thyme

about 1 tsp salt

Many chilli purists don't like the food processor. One minute you have an uneven mixture of chunks and chopped meat and vegetables, a few seconds later you have mush. But the food processor provides a solution for chilli-lovers who don't have a meat grinder, don't live near a shop that sells chilli-grind meat, and don't have the time to cut the meat painstakingly into tiny cubes. The secret is to use the pulse button and to chop in very short bursts. Add the onions, garlic and jalapeños first, and process very briefly, then add the meat. If the seeds and veins are not removed from the jalapeños, this will be hot chilli. For a milder chilli, remove some or all of the seeds and veins. For extra flavour, substitute canned chipotle chillies for the jalapeños.

● Cut the onion into eighths. Peel the garlic and cut each clove in half. Remove the stems from the jalapeños and cut into quarters. Remove any excess fat from the beef and cut beef into 8 or 10 chunks. Put the vegetables in food processor and pulse in two short bursts so vegetables are only partly chopped. Add the beef. Process in short bursts until the beef is coarsely chopped. A few large pieces of vegetable may need to be cut up by hand.

● Heat 1 tablespoon of the oil in a large frying pan and cook half the beef-vegetable mixture until the meat is browned. Put the cooked mixture in a large saucepan and set aside. Heat the remaining oil and cook the remaining beef-vegetable mixture. Add it to the saucepan. Add the beef stock and tomato sauce. Bring to the boil, reduce heat. Add the spices and herbs, but not salt, and stir well. Simmer the chilli for 1½ hours, adding water or beef stock if needed. Taste, add salt and adjust seasonings.

▲ *Cuisinart Chilli*

Double Chilli Chicken and Beef Chilli

MAKES 10 TO 12 SERVINGS

ingredients

2 chicken half-breasts, skin and excess fat removed

2 chicken stock cubes

about 4 tbsp vegetable oil

900 g/2 lb beef, cubed

900 g/2 lb ground beef

3 medium onions, chopped

8 garlic cloves, minced

10 dried chilli pods

250-ml/8-fl oz can tomato sauce

5 tsp ground cumin

4 tsp dried oregano

25 g/1 oz chilli powder

2 tsp unsweetened cocoa

2–3 tsp salt

With dried chilli pods and chilli powder, this chilli has lots of chilli flavour. Shredded chicken, ground beef and cubed beef give it its hearty character. The heat will depend on the type of chilli pods you use. California chillies will produce a mild chilli, while New Mexico chillies will produce a fiery stew. I like to use a mix of California, ancho and New Mexico chillies for a hot but not incendiary chilli.

● Put the chicken breasts in a medium saucepan. Cover with water, bring to the boil and cook for 40 minutes. Remove the chicken from the liquid and refrigerate the chicken. Pour the chicken liquid into a large pan, add the stock cubes and simmer over low heat.

● Heat 1–2 tablespoons of the oil in a large frying pan and cook the cubed beef (cook in batches if necessary) until lightly browned. Add to the chicken stock. Next, brown the ground beef, drain off fat and add the beef to the chicken stock. Heat the remaining oil in the pan and sauté the onions and garlic for 5 minutes. Add to the chilli.

● Remove the stems and seeds from the chilli pods and cut the pods into several pieces. Put in a narrow, deep heatproof bowl and pour 450 ml/¾ pt boiling water over the chillies. Stir to be sure all the chilli pieces are covered by water. Let stand for 30 minutes.

● Remove the chicken from the refrigerator. Shred the chicken and add to the chilli with the tomato sauce.

● Pour the chillies and their soaking liquid into blender or food processor. Purée until smooth. Strain the sauce to remove seeds and bits of skin. Discard solids. Add the sauce to the chilli. Add the remaining ingredients, except salt. Simmer, adding water if needed, until the cubed beef is very tender, about 1½ hours. Taste, adjust seasonings, and add salt.

Old West "Jerky" Chilli

MAKES 4 SERVINGS

This chilli is similar to the chilli eaten in the Old West. It is made with beef "jerky", dried and seasoned beef that kept well on the trail, and pure chilli powders. Because the meat is dried, it will absorb more water than other chillies, so should be checked frequently and water added when needed. Most "jerky" is heavily salted, so little or no additional salt will be needed. That's also why pure chilli powders are used, rather than commercial chilli powder mixes, which contain salt.

● Chop the "jerky" into small pieces, remembering that the pieces will swell as they absorb water. Heat the dripping and cook the garlic and cumin for 1 minute. Add the "jerky" and cook for 3 minutes. Add 450 ml/¾ pt water, the chilli powders, onion flakes and oregano.

● Bring to the boil, reduce heat and simmer. Check often and add water as needed. Simmer for at least 2 hours, then taste and adjust seasonings. To thicken the chilli, mix the flour, masa or cornmeal with 2 tablespoons cold water to make a paste, then add the paste to the chilli. Cook, stirring, until thickened.

▼ Old West "Jerky" Chilli

ingredients

- **175 g/6 oz beef "jerky"**
- **3 tbsp bacon dripping**
- **2 garlic cloves, minced**
- **1 tsp whole cumin seed**
- **2 tbsp California or mild New Mexico chilli powder**
- **2 tbsp hot New Mexico chilli powder**
- **1 tbsp dried onion flakes**
- **1 tsp dried oregano**
- **2 tbsp flour, masa harina or cornmeal**

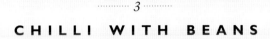

CHILLI WITH BEANS

Despite the insistence of chilli purists that chilli never includes beans, most of us were introduced to chilli by way of a canned concoction of ground beef and beans. Many people who consider themselves chilli-lovers have never had a true, no-beans bowl of Texas Red. Beans stretch the meat in chilli; they also offer a balance to the spice and texture of the meaty stew. For people who believe beans are integral to chilli, we offer the following 22 recipes.

Hayes' Venison and Black Bean Chilli

MAKES 4 TO 6 SERVINGS

ingredients

2–3 tbsp olive oil

2–4 garlic cloves, minced

450 g/1 lb venison tenderloin, cut in thin strips

1 tbsp powdered beef stock cube

garlic salt, black pepper, ground cayenne, ground cumin, crushed red pepper, to taste

1 large white onion, chopped

1 large green pepper, chopped

2–4 fresh hot chillies, preferably serrano or Thai, chopped

450-g/1-lb can black beans, undrained

2 T 425-g/15-oz cans whole tomatoes, undrained

*H*ayes Johnson is a quintessential chilli maker, and a teller of tall tales. The first time I met him, he introduced himself as a chillihead and bragged about the Scotch bonnet chillies growing in pots on his patio. Hayes offered this recipe for "killer chilli" as proof that his chilli-making prowess is more than another tall tale. Hayes recommends serving this chilli with Mexican cornbread and cold beer. Beef can substitute for the venison.

● Heat the olive oil in a deep iron frying pan and sauté the garlic over medium-high heat until it begins to brown. Add the venison and mix well to distribute the garlic. Stir frequently, cooking until all sides are brown. Add the beef stock. Add the spices to taste – don't be shy – and then stir in the chopped vegetables. Stir until coated with oil and beginning to soften.

● Stir the undrained beans and tomatoes into the mixture and bring to a rigorous boil. Stir frequently and boil over medium heat for about 15 minutes. Reduce the heat to medium-low and cover the pan. Simmer for 45–60 minutes, or until meat is tender and sauce is thick. If possible, cook for several hours, or even a day, before needed. The chilli gets better as it gets older.

Stretch-your-beef Chilli Beans

MAKES 6 SERVINGS

This economical chilli uses only a small amount of beef, with kidney beans and lots of vegetables giving it substance. It is a thick, hot chilli, but can be made milder by removing the veins and seeds from the jalapeños.

● Drain the kidney beans, put them in a large pan and cover with water. Bring to the boil, reduce heat and simmer.

● Heat 1 tablespoon of the oil in a frying pan and brown the meat. Add the meat to the beans, discarding fat. Heat the remaining 2 tablespoons oil in the pan and sauté the onion, celery, green pepper and garlic for 5 minutes. Add the vegetables to the beans. Add the remaining ingredients, except salt. Bring to the boil, reduce heat and simmer for at least 1½ hours, adding water if needed. Add salt to taste.

ingredients

175 g/6 oz dried kidney beans, picked over and soaked overnight

3 tbsp vegetable oil

350 g/12 oz beef, cut into 5-mm/¼-in dice

1½ onions, chopped

2 celery sticks, chopped

1 small green pepper, diced

4 garlic cloves, minced

425-g/15-oz can tomatoes, chopped

250 ml/8 fl oz can tomato sauce

3 jalapeño chillies, unseeded, minced

1 tsp ground cumin

1 tsp dried oregano

1 tsp paprika

½ tsp ground coriander

2–3 beef stock cubes, crumbled

1–2 tsp salt

Chunky Pork Chilli with Beans

This hearty chilli is mildly spicy but full of flavour.

1 tbsp vegetable oil

900 g/2 lb pork shoulder, trimmed and cubed

1 onion, chopped

1 celery stick, chopped

450 ml/¾ pt tomato sauce

2 tbsp chilli powder

2 tsp ground cumin

1 tsp dried oregano

350 ml/12 fl oz beer

100 g/4 oz canned green chillies, chopped

1 tsp sugar

1 tsp salt

2 T 450-g/1-lb cans kidney beans

● Heat the oil in a large pan and brown the meat lightly on all sides. Add the onion and celery and cook for 5 minutes. Add the tomato sauce, spices, oregano, beer and chillies.

● Bring the mixture to the boil. Cover, reduce heat and simmer 1¼ hours, stirring occasionally and adding water if necessary. Add the sugar, salt and beans, and cook for 10 minutes. Taste and adjust seasonings.

White Chilli with Chicken

This is a low-fat, moderately spicy chilli, made with chicken, white beans and Anaheim chillies.

350 g/12 oz white beans, picked over and soaked overnight

1 tbsp chilli powder

½ tsp ground cumin

½ tsp dried thyme

½ tsp dried oregano

½ tsp cayenne

½ tsp garlic powder

1 tbsp flour

3 chicken half-breasts, cut into 12-mm/½-in cubes

2 tbsp vegetable oil

1 onion, chopped

1 celery stick, chopped

450 ml/¾ pt chicken stock

4 Anaheim chillies, roasted, peeled and chopped, or 100-g/4-oz can chopped green chillies

about 1 tsp salt

15 g/½ oz fresh coriander, chopped

● Drain the beans, put them in a large pan and barely cover with fresh water. Bring to the boil, reduce heat and simmer.

● Mix the spices, herbs, seasonings and flour. Toss the spice mix with the cubed chicken so the meat is evenly coated with spices, set aside. Heat 1 tablespoon of the oil in a frying pan and sauté the onion and celery for 6 minutes. Add the vegetables to the beans. Heat the remaining oil in a frying pan and cook the chicken, turning often, until all sides are lightly browned. Add the chicken to the beans with the chicken stock and chillies. Simmer until the beans are tender, about 1½ hours total, adding water or chicken stock if needed. Add salt to taste and adjust seasonings. Add the coriander just before serving.

▶ *White Chilli with Chicken*

Chilli Beans with Hamburger

MAKES 4 SERVINGS

ingredients

450 g/1 lb lean ground beef

1 medium onion, chopped

1 celery stick, chopped

½ green pepper, chopped

1 garlic clove, minced

1 tbsp chilli powder

1 tsp dried oregano

½ tsp cayenne

400-g/14-oz can tomatoes, chopped

250-ml/8-fl oz can tomato sauce

425-g/15-g can kidney beans

*T*his simple chilli is similar to canned chilli con carne with ground beef and beans, only better. It is a hot chilli, although not fiery.

● Brown the beef in a frying pan. Remove the meat and set aside. Discard all but 1 tablespoon fat. Add the vegetables to the fat and sauté for 5 minutes. Add the garlic, and sauté for 1 minute. Put the vegetables and beef in a saucepan with the chilli powder, oregano, cayenne, tomatoes and tomato sauce. Mix well, bring to the boil, reduce heat and simmer for 15 minutes. Add the beans and 1 teaspoon salt. Cook for 5 minutes. Taste and adjust seasonings.

Bob French's Colorado Chilli

MAKES 6 SERVINGS

ingredients

350 g/12 oz dry Colorado frijoles, picked over

100 g/4 oz salt pork

1 link (about 100 g/4 oz) mild Italian sausage

450 g/1 lb ground beef

¾ medium onion, chopped

1 garlic clove, minced

2 tbsp chilli powder

1 tbsp flour

1 tsp salt

½ tsp ground cumin

½ tsp sugar

250-ml/8-fl oz can tomato sauce

250 ml/8 fl oz beer

3 shakes of Tabasco sauce

1 green pepper, diced

1 fresh Anaheim chilli, diced

*B*ob French is a transplanted Coloradoan, now living in Florida, who is reminded of home when he makes this moderately spicy chilli, which he recommends serving with cornbread. He and his wife, Virginia, also make this chilli without the beans and pour it over the top of lightly scrambled eggs. Colorado frijoles are small red beans.

● Rinse and drain the beans. Add the beans and salt pork to 2 1/3½ pt water in a large pan. Bring to the boil and boil for 2 minutes. Remove from heat and partially cover with a lid. Leave for 1 hour. Bring to the boil again and then reduce heat to simmer. Cover tightly and simmer for 1 hour. Drain, saving about 450 ml/¾ pt of the bean liquid.

● Cut off the end of the Italian sausage and squeeze out the sausagemeat. Break up the meat into a frying pan and brown it with the beef. Drain off the fat. If the pan is large enough, add the beans and remaining ingredients, except bean liquid. Otherwise, transfer the meat to the bean pan and add the beans and remaining ingredients, except bean liquid. Heat and add the bean liquid as needed. Simmer for at least 1 hour.

▶ *Bob French's Colorado Chilli*

Ground Turkey Chilli with Black Beans

MAKES 4 TO 6 SERVINGS

Made with a combination of fresh and dried chillies, this is a hot chilli.

ingredients

- 2 ancho chillies
- 2 dried Anaheim chillies
- 450 g/1 lb ground turkey
- 250 ml/8 fl oz chicken stock
- 2 tbsp vegetable oil
- 1 medium onion, chopped
- 1 celery stick, chopped
- 2 fresh jalapeño or serrano chillies, unseeded, minced
- 425-g/15-oz can tomatoes, chopped
- ¼ tsp dried sage
- 1 tsp dried oregano
- 425-g/15-oz can black beans
- about 1 tsp salt

● Cut the dried chillies in half and remove the stems and seeds. Put them in a small heatproof bowl. Pour 250 ml/ 8 fl oz boiling water over the chillies, making sure all parts are immersed. Leave chillies to soak about for 30 minutes while you prepare other ingredients.

● Crumble and brown the turkey in a frying pan. Drain fat, if needed. Put the turkey in a large saucepan with the chicken stock and simmer. Heat the oil in a frying pan and sauté the onion and celery for 5 minutes. Add the vegetables, along with the fresh chillies, tomatoes, sage and oregano. Let the turkey simmer.

● Pour the dried chillies and their soaking water into a blender or food processor. Purée until a thick red sauce forms. Strain the sauce to remove seeds and bits of skin. Discard the solids. Add the sauce to the turkey. Simmer the turkey for 15 minutes, adding water or chicken stock if needed. Add the beans and salt to taste, and heat through.

Cheesy Chilli Beans

This is a homey, substantial chilli. Melting the cheese in the pot cuts the sharpness of the cheese and mellows the heat of the chilli. The chilli's spiciness will depend on the amount of cayenne used.

● Heat the oil in a frying pan and sauté the onion, celery and garlic for 5 minutes, then remove to large saucepan. Add the chopped tomato, beef stock and tomato sauce.

● Brown the ground beef in the frying pan and add to the vegetable mixture. Stir in the chilli powder, cumin and cayenne. Simmer for about 30 minutes, adding a small amount of water or beef stock if needed. Add the beans and salt, then taste and adjust seasonings, keeping in mind that the cheese will add salt. Add the cheese and cook, stirring well, just until the cheese is melted and well blended.

ingredients

2 tbsp vegetable oil

1 onion, chopped

1 celery stick, minced

2 garlic cloves, minced

1 medium tomato, peeled and chopped

250 ml/8 fl oz beef stock

250-ml/8-fl oz can tomato sauce

450 g/1 lb ground beef

1 tbsp chilli powder

1 tsp ground cumin

¼–1 tsp cayenne

425-g/15-oz can kidney beans, drained

about 1 tsp salt

225 g/8 oz mature Cheddar cheese, grated

Tailgate Chilli

This is a moderately spicy chilli that will feed a small crowd. It uses three meats – hot pork sausage, and coarsely ground beef and pork. If you can't get coarsely ground meat from your grocer and don't have the equipment to do it at home, use lean hamburger for the beef, and cube the pork. This is not a sweet or Cincinnati-style chilli. The small amount of allspice adds just another note of flavour, while the honey helps tame the bitterness of the chilli powder.

ingredients

450 g/1 lb dried pink or red beans, picked over and soaked overnight

about 4 tablespoons vegetable oil

3 medium onions, chopped

8 garlic cloves, minced

1 celery stick, finely chopped

½ green pepper, finely chopped

450 g/1 lb hot pork sausage

450 g/1 lb pork, coarsely ground

900 g/2 lb beef, coarsely ground

425-g/15-oz can tomatoes, chopped

250-ml/8-fl oz can tomato sauce

2 beef stock cubes

50 g/2 oz chilli powder

1–2 tbsp hot New Mexico chilli powder

1 tbsp ground cumin

2 tsp dried oregano

2 tsp dried basil

½ tsp ground allspice

1 tsp honey

2–4 tsp salt

● Rinse the beans and put them in a large pan. Add enough water to cover the beans by 5 cm/2 in. Bring the beans to the boil, reduce heat and simmer.

● Heat 2 tablespoons of the oil in a large frying pan and sauté the onion, garlic, celery and green pepper for 5 minutes. Add to the beans. Cook the pork sausage, chopping large clumps, until lightly browned. Tilt the pan to drain the fat and remove the sausage with a slotted spoon. Add the sausage to beans.

Discard fat or use 1 tablespoon to cook the pork.

● Heat 1 tablespoon vegetable oil or sausage fat and cook the pork until lightly browned. Add to the beans. Heat the remaining vegetable oil and brown the beef. (If necessary, cook the beef in two batches.) Add the browned beef to the beans with the remaining ingredients, except salt. Simmer until the beans are tender, about 1½ hours. Taste and adjust seasonings. Add salt to taste.

Olé Molé Pork Chilli

T his is a moderately hot chilli that uses the relatively new "hot" or "Mexican" chilli powder, available in most supermarket spice sections. Hot chilli powder is a mix of ground chillies and other spices, but is hotter than traditional chilli powder. This is a meaty chilli in a rich sauce. The secret ingredient is molé paste, available in Mexican speciality grocers and some well-stocked supermarkets.

● Drain, rinse and drain the beans. Put them in a large pan and cover with water. Bring to the boil, reduce heat and simmer.
● Heat 1 tablespoon of the oil in a large frying pan and cook the pork until browned. Remove the pork with a slotted spoon and add to the beans. Discard the greasy cooking liquids. Heat the remaining oil in the pan and sauté the onion and garlic for 5 minutes, then add to the beans. Add the remaining ingredients, except salt. Cook until the meat and beans are tender, 1½–2 hours. Add salt, taste and adjust seasonings.

ingredients

175 g/6 oz black beans, picked over and soaked overnight

2 tbsp vegetable oil

900 g/2 lb pork, cubed

1½ medium onions, chopped

2 garlic cloves, minced

1 beef stock cube

250-ml/8-fl oz can tomato sauce

1 tbsp hot or Mexican chilli powder

2 tbsp chilli powder

2 tsp dried oregano

1 tsp celery salt

1 tsp molé paste

about 1 tsp salt

Easy Salsa Chilli

T his is a quick and easy chilli, made with bottled salsa and dried onions. Use the salsa of your choice – it will determine how hot the chilli is. To make the chilli hotter, add ½ teaspoon more Tabasco or other hot pepper sauce.

● Soak the onion flakes in 120 ml/4 fl oz water. Brown the meat in a frying pan and drain off excess fat. Add the salsa, chilli powder, cumin, oregano and garlic powder to the meat, stir well. Add the onion and soaking water. Simmer the mixture for 10–15 minutes, until the chilli is soupy but not watery. Drain the beans, reserving the liquid. Add the beans to the chilli, then add bean liquid as needed. Heat for 5 minutes. Add salt, taste and adjust seasonings.

ingredients

2 tbsp dried onion flakes

450 g/1 lb ground beef

450-ml/¾ pt bottle red salsa

1 tbsp chilli powder

1 tsp ground cumin

1 tsp dried oregano

½ tsp garlic powder

425-g/15-oz can kidney beans

about ½ tsp salt

Chorizo and Black Bean Chilli

ingredients

350 g/12 oz black beans, picked over and soaked overnight

450 ml/¾ pt beef stock

2 tbsp vegetable oil

175 g/6 oz chopped onion

1 small green pepper, diced

2 garlic cloves, minced

175-ml/6-fl oz can tomato purée

2 tbsp chilli powder

¼ tsp cayenne

1 tsp ground cumin

1 tsp dried oregano

450 g/1 lb chorizo sausage (not smoked)

50 g/2 oz spring onion, chopped

25 g/1 oz fresh coriander, chopped

100 g/4 oz Cheddar cheese, grated

1–2 tsp salt

This chilli stretches a lb of chorizo sausage into a substantial meal for six to eight people. It is a moderately spicy chilli of complex flavour – the nutty flavour of black beans, the Spanish sausage of pork and paprika, a mix of fresh jalapeños with cayenne and chilli powder, plus the mellowing influence of jack cheese. The last-minute addition of spring onions and fresh coriander adds texture. With ¼ teaspoon cayenne, it is moderately spicy – add more for a hotter chilli.

● Drain, rinse and drain the beans. Put them in a large pan and cover with water. Add the beef stock, bring to the boil, reduce heat and simmer.

● Heat the oil in a frying pan and sauté the onion, green pepper and garlic for 5 minutes. Add to the beans. Add the tomato purée and seasonings. Continue to let the beans simmer, adding water or stock if needed.

● When the beans have cooked for about 1 hour, crumble the chorizo into a frying pan. Fry until the meat is cooked and the fat is rendered out. With a slotted spoon remove the meat – taking care to drain the fat – and add it to the beans. Discard the fat.

● Continue simmering the beans until tender, a total of 1½–2 hours. Five minutes before serving, add the spring onion and coriander. Add salt, taste and adjust seasonings. Immediately before serving, stir in the cheese, so it is only partially melted when served.

Smokin' Chipotle Turkey Chilli

MAKES 4 TO 6 SERVINGS

This is a hot chilli stew with the delicious, smoky flavour of chipotle chillies. If you have leftover turkey from a holiday bird, no one will complain about being served turkey yet another time. Add a third chipotle chilli for a really hot dish. If you cannot find Rotel tomatoes, use standard canned tomatoes plus one chopped Anaheim chilli, canned or fresh.

● Heat the oil in a frying pan and sauté the garlic and onion for 5 minutes. Put the vegetables in a large saucepan with the chicken stock and turkey. Bring to the boil. Add the remaining ingredients, except the beans and salt. Reduce the heat and simmer for at least 30 minutes, up to 1 hour, adding water or chicken stock if needed. Add the beans. Taste, add a little salt, and adjust seasonings.

ingredients

2 tbsp vegetable oil

3 garlic cloves, minced

1 onion, chopped

450 ml/¾ pt chicken stock

350 g/12 oz cubed cooked turkey

2–3 minced chipotle chillies

300-g/10-oz can Rotel diced tomatoes with green chillies

250-ml/8-fl oz can tomato sauce

3 tbsp chilli powder

1 tsp each of: ground cumin, celery salt, ground coriander, unsweetened cocoa

450-g/1-lb can pinto or red beans

Chilli with Ground Beef and Hot Italian Sausage

MAKES 6 SERVINGS

This is a moderately hot chilli, accented by the flavours of the Italian sausage.

● Drain, rinse and drain the beans. Put them in a large saucepan and add water to cover by 5 cm/2 in. Bring to the boil, reduce heat and simmer.

● Crumble the beef and sausage into a large frying pan and cook until browned. Remove the meat and add to the beans. Discard the fat, or, if it is not watery, save 2 tablespoons for sautéing the vegetables and discard the rest.

● Reheat the sausage fat or heat the oil and sauté the onion, celery, and garlic for 5 minutes. Add to the beans with the remaining ingredients, except salt. Simmer until the beans are tender, a total of at least 1½ hours, adding water if needed. When the beans are tender, add salt, taste and adjust seasonings.

ingredients

175 g/6 oz dried pinto beans, picked over and soaked overnight

450 g/1 lb ground beef

225 g/8 oz hot Italian-style sausage

2 tbsp vegetable oil, if needed

1 onion, chopped

1 celery stick, chopped

2 garlic cloves, minced

2 tbsp chilli powder

1 tsp dried oregano

1 tsp dried basil

½ tsp cayenne

100-g/4-oz can chopped green chillies

250-ml/8-fl oz can tomato sauce

about 1 tsp salt

Double Turkey Chilli with Green Chillies

ingredients

6 large Anaheim chillies

1 tbsp vegetable oil

450 g/1 lb uncooked turkey meat, cubed

175 g/6 oz turkey sausage

1 medium onion, chopped

1 celery stick, finely chopped

2 garlic cloves, minced

750 ml/1¼ pt chicken stock

425-g/15-oz can tomatoes

½ tsp cayenne or to taste

425-g/15-oz can white or kidney beans

1–2 tsp salt

Turkey and turkey sausage can provide a lower-cholesterol alternative to traditional beef and pork chillies. Check the turkey sausage, however, as some products include a high percentage of turkey fat and skin. Any part of the turkey can provide the cubed turkey. The easiest but priciest alternative is using turkey cutlets. This is a substantial chilli with a savoury, moderately spicy sauce. It is made with mild green Anaheim chillies, and the heat is provided by cayenne, but other green chillies can be substituted.

● Roast the chillies under a grill, turning, until skin on all sides is blistered and mostly blackened. Put the chillies in a paper bag or covered bowl to steam.

● Heat the oil in a large frying pan, add the turkey meat and crumble in the turkey sausage. Cook until browned. Add the onion, celery and garlic, and cook for 5 minutes. Put the meat and vegetables in a large saucepan with the chicken stock. Bring to the boil, reduce heat and simmer.

● Peel the blackened skins from the chillies and remove the stems and seeds. Chop half the chillies and add to the stew. Cut the three remaining chillies in several large pieces. Put the chillies and tomatoes in a blender or food processor with as much of the tomato liquid as is needed and purée. Add the tomato-chilli purée, and any remaining tomato liquid, to the chilli. Add the cayenne.

● When the chilli has simmered at least 45 minutes, add the beans and cook for 5 minutes. Add the salt, taste and adjust seasonings.

Pork Chilli with Italian Sausage

Fennel in the Italian sausage adds a pleasing accent to this moderately hot chilli.

ingredients

450 g/1 lb ground pork

100 g/4 oz Italian sausage

1 tbsp vegetable oil

1 onion, chopped

2 garlic cloves, minced

175-g/6-oz can tomato purée

2 tbsp chilli powder

1 tbsp hot New Mexico chilli powder

1 tsp dried oregano

1 tsp ground cumin

1 tbsp lime juice

450-g/1-lb can pinto beans

about 1 tsp salt

● Brown the pork and sausage in a hot frying pan. Drain off excess fat. Put the meat in a large saucepan and set aside. Heat the oil in the frying pan and sauté the onion and garlic for 5 minutes. Add to the meat with 450 ml/¾ pt water, the tomato purée and seasonings. Mix well and bring to the boil. Reduce heat and simmer about 1¼ hours. Add the lime juice and beans. Simmer for 15 minutes. Add salt, taste, and adjust seasonings.

Pork and Black Bean Chilli with Tomatillos

This is a pleasantly spicy, slightly tart chilli that uses tomatillos instead of tomato sauce. If fresh tomatillos are not available, substitute canned ones, which do not have to be boiled before using.

ingredients

175 g/6 oz dried black beans, picked over and soaked overnight

2 tbsp vegetable oil

900 g/2 lb pork, cubed

1 large onion, chopped

450 g/1 lb tomatillos

2 tsp chicken stock

1 tsp garlic powder

2 tbsp chilli powder

1 tbsp hot New Mexico chilli powder

1 tsp ground cumin

1 tsp dried marjoram

1–2 tsp salt

● Drain the beans, put in a large pan and add enough water to cover by 5 cm/2 in. Bring to the boil, reduce heat and simmer.

● Heat 1 tablespoon of the oil in a large, deep frying pan or big saucepan and cook the pork until lightly browned. Add the pork to the beans. Heat the remaining oil in the pan and sauté the onion for 5 minutes. Add the onion to the beans.

● Boil water in a medium saucepan. Husk and rinse the tomatillos, then add them to the boiling water. Simmer the tomatillos until they are soft, 10–15 minutes. Remove the tomatillos and drain them. Purée the tomatillos in a blender or food processor. Add the purée to the chilli. Add the stock and spices to the chilli. Continue simmering the chilli until the pork has cooked for about 1½ hours, adding water if needed. Add salt, taste and adjust seasonings.

Venison Chilli with Nopalitos

*B*ecause it is very lean, even ground venison needs to be cooked with added fat. The bacon dripping provides extra flavour, but olive oil can be substituted. Venison's strong flavour stands up nicely to hot chillies. Nopalitos, bits of cactus, add flavour reminiscent of green beans. Seek out canned or bottled nopalitos in the speciality sections of high-quality delicatessens or department stores. This chilli is moderately spicy.

● In a large, wide pan, heat the bacon dripping and sauté the onion, green pepper, and garlic for 5 minutes. Add the venison and cook until lightly browned. Add the beer, 450 ml/¾ pt water, and tomato sauce. Stir well, bring to the boil, reduce heat. Mix in the seasonings and simmer for 1 hour. Add the nopalitos and beans. Simmer for 20 minutes. Add salt, taste, and adjust seasonings.

3 tbsp bacon dripping

1 onion, chopped

½ green pepper, finely chopped

3 garlic cloves, minced

575 g/1¼ lb coarsely ground venison

350 ml/12 fl oz beer

250-ml/8-fl oz can tomato sauce

2 tbsp chilli powder

2 tbsp hot or Mexican chilli powder

1 tsp ground cumin

1 tsp dried marjoram

¼ tsp dried thyme

300-g/11-oz jar nopalitos, rinsed, drained and chopped

425-g/15-oz can black beans, undrained

1 tsp salt

Kitchen Sink Chilli

MAKES 12 SERVINGS

This moderately spicy chilli has beef, turkey sausage, tomatoes, mushrooms, olives, beans – everything but the kitchen sink.

ingredients

- 1.4 kg/3 lb ground beef
- 450 g/1 lb turkey sausage
- 3 onions, chopped
- 6 garlic cloves, minced
- ½ green pepper, finely chopped
- 750 ml/1¼ pt beef stock
- 250-ml/8-fl oz can tomato sauce
- 425-g/15-oz can tomatoes, chopped
- 40 g/1½ oz mild chilli molido
- 1 tbsp hot chilli powder
- 1 tbsp ground cumin
- 1 tbsp dried oregano
- ¼ tsp ground allspice
- 175 g/6 oz mushrooms, sliced
- 2 T 50-g/2-oz cans sliced olives
- 3 T 450-g/1-lb cans kidney or pinto beans

● Crumble the beef and sausage into a large stockpot. Cook, chopping any large pieces, until browned. Spoon off and discard the fat. Add 450 ml/¾ pt water and the remain-ing ingredients, except the olives, beans and salt. Stir well, bring to the boil, then reduce heat. Simmer for 1 hour, stirring occasionally and adding water if needed. Add the olives and beans, and simmer for 15 minutes. Add some salt, taste and adjust seasonings.

4

UNTRADITIONAL
CHILLIES

If it wasn't bad enough that people spoiled the purity of good chilli by adding beans, some cooks went further. Some cookbooks include chillies made with sauerkraut, raisins, pumpkin and other truly odd ingredients. For those with an adventurous palate, here are eight chillies that stretch the standard, from Sissy Chilli for the Gourmet Palate (sun-dried tomatoes, olives, goat cheese) to Slightly Seedy Chilli (toasted sesame and caraway seeds) to that midwestern favourite, Cincinnati Five-way Chilli, seasoned with turmeric, cardamom and cinnamon, and served over spaghetti.

Slightly Seedy Chilli

ingredients

2 tbsp vegetable oil

1 onion, chopped

3 garlic cloves, minced

1 celery stick, finely chopped

¼ green pepper, finely chopped

450 g/1 lb ground beef

2 beef stock cubes

425-g/15-oz can tomatoes, chopped

250-ml/8-fl oz can tomato sauce

3 tbsp chilli powder

1 tbsp hot New Mexico chilli powder

½–1 tsp crushed red chilli flakes

1 tsp caraway seeds

1 tbsp sesame seeds

450-g/1-lb can kidney beans

½–1 tsp salt

This looks and tastes – at least initially – like a typical chilli of moderate heat. But there is a note of nutty flavour with just the faintest hint of sweetness, added by the toasted sesame and caraway seeds, which are not quite recognizable.

● Heat the oil in a frying pan and sauté the onion, garlic, celery and green pepper for 5 minutes. Put vegetables in a large saucepan and set aside. Add the beef to the frying pan and cook until browned. Drain off fat and add the beef to the vegetables. Dissolve the stock cubes in 250 ml/8 fl oz boiling water. Add to the beef with 450 ml/¾ pt water. Stir and bring to the boil. Add the tomatoes, tomato sauce, chilli powders and chilli flakes. Mix well, reduce heat and simmer.

● Put the seeds in a small, dry frying pan over medium heat toast, shaking frequently so they don't scorch, until the sesame seeds are golden. Add to the chilli. Simmer for about 1 hour, then add the beans, plus liquid if needed. Taste, add salt and adjust seasonings.

Sissy Chilli for the Gourmet Palate

MAKES 4 SERVINGS

Ingredients in this mildly spicy chilli are a bit unusual – goat's cheese, sun-dried tomatoes and black olives. A chilli-lover with an asbestos palate would scorn it as something for sissies, but it's truly delicious. Sun-dried tomatoes give it a bit of tang and an interesting texture, olives add a touch of sweetness and the strong flavour of goat's cheese balances the spicy flavour. For a somewhat hotter chilli, don't remove the jalapeños' seeds and veins. It is easier to cut the sun-dried tomatoes with kitchen scissors than it is to chop them – remember the pieces will swell as they absorb cooking liquids.

● Heat 1 tablespoon of the oil in a large frying pan and sauté the onion and garlic for 5 minutes. Heat the remaining oil in the pan and cook the beef until lightly browned. Put the vegetables and beef in a saucepan. Add the beef stock, 450 ml/¾ pt water, tomato sauce and seasonings. Bring to the boil, reduce heat and simmer for 1 hour.

● Add the sun-dried tomatoes and chillies. Simmer for 30 minutes. Add the olives, coriander, and salt, taste, and adjust seasonings. Ladle into bowls and sprinkle the goat's cheese over the chilli.

ingredients

- **2 tbsp olive oil**
- **1 medium onion, chopped**
- **4 garlic cloves, minced**
- **900 g/2 lb beef, cubed**
- **450 ml/¾ pt beef stock**
- **250-ml/8-fl oz can tomato sauce**
- **2 tbsp chilli powder**
- **1 tsp dried oregano**
- **1 tsp dried basil**
- **¼ tsp dried rosemary, crushed**
- **75 g/3 oz sun-dried tomatoes, coarsely chopped**
- **2 jalapeño chillies, seeded and minced**
- **50-g/2-oz can sliced olives**
- **3 tbsp fresh coriander, chopped**
- **about ½ tsp salt**
- **50–75 g/2–3 oz goat's cheese, crumbled**

Garlicky Pork Chilli

MAKES 6 SERVINGS

ingredients

175 g/6 oz dried black beans, picked over and soaked overnight

16 garlic cloves

about 4 tbsp olive oil

450 ml/¾ pt chicken stock

1 medium onion, chopped

900 g/2 lb pork, diced

1 tsp ground cumin

1 tsp paprika

1 tsp dried oregano

250-ml/8-fl oz can tomato sauce

1 tbsp mild New Mexico chilli powder

1 tbsp ancho chilli powder

about 1 tsp salt

Mild New Mexico and moderate ancho chilli powders provide the background for the delicious garlic flavour of this pork and black bean chilli. California chilli powder can be substituted if you can't find mild New Mexico chilli powder.

● Preheat the oven to 180°C/350°F/Gas Mark 4. Put 8 of the garlic cloves on an 20-cm/8-in square of foil. Brush with 1 tablespoon of the olive oil. Wrap the foil around the garlic to form a sealed bundle. Bake for 35 minutes. Remove from the oven, open the foil and leave to cool.

● Drain the beans. Put in a large pan, add just enough water to cover, then add the chicken stock. Bring to the boil, reduce heat and simmer.

● Heat 1 tablespoon of the oil in a frying pan and sauté the onion for 5 minutes. Add to the beans. Add another 1 tablespoon of the oil to the pan and brown the pork. Add to the beans.

● Mince the remaining garlic cloves. Heat the remaining oil in a very small frying pan and cook the minced garlic, cumin, paprika and oregano, stirring often, for 1 minute. Add to the beans.

● Squeeze the roasted garlic from the papery peel. Add to the beans with the tomato sauce and chilli powders. Stir well and continue cooking until the beans and pork are tender, about 1½ hours total. Add salt and adjust seasonings.

Fried Chicken Chilli

Cubes of chicken are coated with spices, then fried before being added to the chilli stock, giving the meat extra spice. This is a hot chilli that gets balance from the pinto beans.

● Mix the flour with the cayenne, chilli powder, cumin, oregano, garlic powder and salt. Put the mixture in a bag. Add the chicken and shake until the chicken cubes are evenly coated with spice mixture.

● Heat 2 tablespoons of the oil in a large frying pan and cook the chicken, turning as needed, until the chicken is lightly browned on all sides. Set the chicken aside. Heat the remaining oil in the pan and sauté the onion for 5 minutes.

● Put the chicken and onion in a large saucepan with the chicken stock. Add the remaining ingredients, except the beans and salt. Bring to the boil, reduce heat and simmer for about 1 hour, adding water if needed. Add the beans. Taste, add salt and adjust seasonings.

ingredients

2 tbsp flour

¼ tsp cayenne

1 tsp chilli powder

½ tsp ground cumin

½ tsp dried oregano

½ tsp garlic powder

¼ tsp salt

4 chicken half-breasts, cubed

3 tbsp vegetable oil

1 onion, chopped

450 ml/¾ pt chicken stock

26 g/1 oz chilli powder

1 tbsp hot New Mexico chilli powder

1 tsp ground cumin

1 tsp dried oregano

2 u 300-g/10-oz cans pinto beans

about 1 tsp salt

Cincinnati Five-way Chilli

ingredients

900 g/2 lb ground beef

1½ onions, chopped

2 garlic cloves, minced

1 tbsp red wine vinegar

1 tsp cinnamon

½ tsp allspice

¼ tsp ground cloves

¼ tsp ground cardamom

1 tsp dried oregano

½ tsp ground cumin

¼ tsp turmeric (can substitute curry powder)

2 tbsp chilli powder

½ tsp crushed chilli flakes, or more to taste (optional)

175-g/6-oz can tomato purée

about 1 tsp salt

425-g/15-oz can kidney beans

450 g/1 lb spaghetti, cooked

225 g/8 oz Cheddar cheese, grated

1½ onions, chopped (for layer)

*S*ometimes called chilli-mac, Cincinnati Chilli is a Texas purist's nightmare. Not only does it come with tomatoes and beans, but is served on top of spaghetti! There's a bit of eastern Mediterranean influence in the spices, which are truly a potpourri – cinnamon, cloves, cardamom, turmeric, cumin and oregano, in addition to the chilli powder. Typically it's not as hot as more traditional chillies. It's a layered chilli, with the five layers – spaghetti, chilli, beans, chopped onion and grated Cheddar cheese – accounting for its name. But among midwesterners,. Cincinnati Chilli has as many devotees as Texas chilli does in the South West. In this version, optional crushed chilli flakes add the heat.

● In a large pan, brown the ground beef. Add the onion and garlic and cook for 5 minutes. Spoon off any excess fat. Add 750 ml/1¼ pt water, the vinegar, spices and herbs, chilli flakes and tomato purée. Mix well. Bring to the boil, reduce heat and simmer for 2 hours, stirring occasionally and adding water if needed. Just before serving, add salt, taste and adjust seasonings.

● You can heat the kidney beans and serve them on the side, or mix them with the chilli before serving. To serve, begin with a layer of spaghetti, add the chilli, then the beans, cheese and onion.

California Five-way Chilli

MAKES 6 TO 8 SERVINGS

This variation of Cincinnati chilli uses Mexican ingredients that have become staples in Californian kitchens: chorizo sausage, black beans, coriander and a combination of unsweetened cocoa, cinnamon and cloves that are reminiscent of molé dishes. It is pleasantly spicy.

● Brown the ground beef in a frying pan. Spoon off the excess fat, put the meat in large saucepan and set aside. Brown the chorizo sausage in a frying pan. Drain off all but 1 tablespoon of the fat, and remove the sausage with a slotted spoon. Add the sausage to the saucepan. Reheat the fat and sauté the onion and garlic for 5 minutes. Add to the saucepan.

● Add the cocoa and seasonings to the saucepan. Add the vinegar and tomato purée and 450 ml/¾ pt water. Bring the

mixture to the boil, stirring well. Reduce heat and simmer for about 1¼ hours, adding water if necessary. Add the coriander and salt to taste.

● Traditionally, the beans are one of the five layers in five-way chilli, but if you wish to mix the beans into the chilli, do so now.

● To serve, start with a layer of spaghetti, add the chilli, beans, chopped onion and cheese.

ingredients

625 g/1½ lb ground beef

225 g/8 oz chorizo sausage (not smoked)

1 onion, chopped

3 garlic cloves, minced

2 tsp unsweetened cocoa

1 tsp cinnamon

¼ tsp ground cloves

1 tsp ground cumin

1 tsp dried oregano

2 tbsp chilli powder

1 tbsp hot or Mexican chilli powder

1 tbsp red wine vinegar

175-ml/6-fl oz can tomato paste

15 g/½ oz fresh coriander, chopped

about 1 tsp salt

450-g/1-lb can black beans

350 g/12 oz spaghetti, cooked

1½ onions, chopped (for layer)

225 g/8 oz Cheddar cheese, grated

◀ *California Five-way Chilli*

Smoked Turkey Chilli

ingredients

350 g/12 oz frijoles colorados, picked over and soaked overnight

6 large dried chillies

2 tbsp vegetable oil

1½ medium onions, chopped

2 celery sticks, chopped

225–300 g/8-10oz smoked turkey, shredded or chopped

425-g/15-oz can tomatoes, chopped

2 chicken stock cubes

2 tsp dried oregano

1 tsp ground cumin

1 tsp celery salt

1 tsp garlic powder

½ tsp sugar

¼–1 tsp salt

*S*moked turkey is like ham – with beans, it doesn't take a large amount to make this chilli a meaty dish. It is a little soupy. The heat will depend on the type of dried chillies you use, but the smoked turkey stands up well to hot chillies. I like a combination of two New Mexico, two Anaheim, and two chillies negros, which makes a moderately hot chilli. Frijoles colorados are small red beans. One large turkey drumstick will produce nearly 300g/10 oz of chopped meat.

● Drain, rinse and drain the beans. Put them in a large pan and cover them with water. Bring to the boil, reduce heat and simmer.

● Cut the dried chillies in half and remove the stems and seeds. Place the chillies in a small, heatproof bowl and pour 250 ml/8 fl oz boiling water over.

Let them soak for 30 minutes, making sure that all the pieces of chilli are covered with water.

● While the chillies are soaking, heat the oil in a frying pan and sauté the onion and celery for 5 minutes, then add to the beans. Add the turkey, chopped tomatoes, crumbled stock cubes, oregano, cumin, celery salt, garlic powder and sugar to the beans.

● Put the chillies and their soaking water in a blender or food processor. Purée until a smooth red-brown sauce forms. Strain the sauce to remove seeds and bits of skin; discard the solids. Add the sauce to the beans.

● Simmer the chilli, adding water if needed, until the beans are tender, at least 1½ hours. Add salt, taste and adjust seasonings.

◀ *Smoked Turkey Chilli*

Marinated Chicken Chilli with Mushrooms and Green Chillies

MAKES 4 TO 5 SERVINGS

This is a mild chilli, made with chicken that has been marinated in a spicy vinaigrette.

● Combine the vinaigrette, 2 garlic cloves, coriander and cumin, and shake well. Put the chicken in a sealable plastic bag or a plastic bowl with a lid. Pour the vinaigrette over the chicken and stir well so all pieces are coated. Let the chicken marinate in the refrigerator at least 2 hours or as long as overnight.

● Heat 1 tablespoon of the oil in a frying pan and sauté the onion and remaining garlic for 5 minutes. Put in a large saucepan with the chicken stock, oregano and 250 ml/8 fl oz water. Heat another tablespoon oil in the frying pan. Drain and discard the excess marinade from the chicken. Sauté the chicken cubes until lightly browned. Add to the chicken stock. Bring to the boil, reduce heat and simmer.

● Roast the chillies under the grill, turning often until they are charred on all sides. Remove from the grill and put in a bag. Close the bag and let the chillies steam for at least 10 minutes. Remove them from the bag, cut off and discard the stems and seeds. Peel and discard the blackened skin. Put half the chillies in blender or food processor with a little liquid from the pot and purée. Add the purée to the saucepan. Chop the remaining chillies and add them to the saucepan.

● Heat the remaining oil and sauté the mushrooms for 10 minutes. Add them to the chilli. After the chicken has simmered for 1 hour, add salt, taste and adjust seasonings.

ingredients

5 tbsp bottled vinaigrette

3 garlic cloves, minced

2 tbsp fresh coriander, chopped

½ tsp ground cumin

4 chicken half-breasts, cubed

4 tbsp olive oil

1 medium onion, chopped

450 ml/¾ pt chicken stock

1 tsp dried oregano

6 poblano chillies, or 3 poblanos and 3 Anaheims

175 g/6 oz mushrooms, sliced

about 1 tsp salt

ALIAS CHILLI

It is hard to draw the line between what is a chilli and what's not. As long as we are defining chilli liberally, here are six stews of meat and chilli that are known by other names, but could be considered chillies as well. They range from Feijoada, a garlicky Brazilian stew of pork and black beans, to Bredie, a South African stew of mutton, tomato juice and beans.

Feijoada

MAKES 8 TO 10 SERVINGS

ingredients

350 g/12 oz dried black beans, picked over and soaked overnight

4 tbsp vegetable oil

3 dried chillies de arbol, whole

8 garlic cloves, minced

900 g/2 lb pork loin, cubed

1 large onion, chopped

425-g/15-oz can tomatoes, chopped

450 g/1 lb linguica, cut into 5-mm/¼-in slices

3 jalapeño chillies, unseeded, minced

about 2 tsp salt

Feijoada, a spicy stew of black beans and pork, is the ceremonial dish of Brazil. Traditionally it is made with various parts of the pig, such as snout, ears, tail and feet. This hot Americanized version uses pork loin and linguica, a garlicky Portuguese sausage. Serve Feijoada with rice, greens and orange slices. If you cannot find chillies de arbol, any small hot dried red chillies will do.

● Drain the beans, put them in a stockpot and add enough water to cover 5 cm/ 2 in. Bring to the boil, reduce heat and simmer.

● Heat 1 tablespoon of the oil in a small frying pan and sauté the chillies de arbol and half the minced garlic for 1–2 minutes, until the garlic just starts to brown. Add to the beans. Heat another 1 tablespoon oil in a large frying pan and cook the pork until lightly browned. Add the pork to the beans. Heat the remaining oil in a frying pan and sauté the onion and remaining half of the minced garlic for 5 minutes, then add to the beans.

● Add the tomatoes and linguica to the beans. Return the stew to the boil, reduce heat and simmer. When beans have simmered for 1 hour, add the jalapeños. Continue simmering until the beans are tender, a total of 1½–2 hours. Add salt, taste and adjust seasonings.

◀ *Feijoada*

Carnitas Chilli

MAKES 4 SERVINGS

*C*arnitas, a Mexican dish, are little chunks of meat served with a hot sauce for dipping, or shredded, mixed with sauce and used as a filling for enchiladas. This hot version mixes the shredded twice-cooked meat and sauce to make a chilli-like stew. Serve it with rice or warm tortillas.

● Combine the chilli powder, cumin, oregano, garlic and onion powders. Put in a bag with the pork chunks. Shake until the meat is evenly covered, then use your fingers to rub it in. Leave at room temperature for 45 minutes to absorb the spice flavours. Heat 2 tablespoons of the oil in a Dutch oven or other large, ovenproof casserole and brown the meat on all sides, turning often so the spices do not scorch. Add the onion pieces and enough water to cover the meat. Bring to the boil, reduce heat and simmer, covered, for 1½ hours. Preheat the oven to 180°C/350°F/Gas Mark 4. Put the casserole in the oven and bake, uncovered, for 45 minutes.

● While the meat is in the oven, prepare the chillies. Remove the stems and seeds and cut each chilli into 4 pieces. Put the chillies in a narrow deep bowl. Boil the beef stock and pour over the chillies. Stir so all pieces are soaking. Let the chillies soak for 30 minutes. Meanwhile, heat the remaining oil in a frying pan and sauté the onion for 10 minutes. Set aside. Pour the chillies and their soaking liquid into a blender or food processor. Purée until a smooth sauce forms. Strain to remove seeds and the bits of skin, discard the solids. Combine the sauce with the sautéed onion.

● When the meat has cooked for 45 minutes, remove from the oven. Pour any remaining liquids into the chilli sauce. Let the meat stand until it is cool enough to handle. Shred the meat. Heat the chilli sauce and stir in the meat. Add salt to taste.

ingredients

1 tbsp chilli powder

2 tsp ground cumin

2 tsp dried oregano

1 tsp garlic powder

1 tsp onion powder

900 g/2 lb pork loin, cut into 8 or 10 chunks

3 tbsp vegetable oil

1 onion, cut into eighths

6 large dried red chillies, preferably New Mexico or chillies negros or a combination

250 ml/8 fl oz beef stock

1 medium onion, chopped

about 1 tsp salt

ingredients

2 lamb shanks

2 bay leaves

175 g/6 oz dried pinto beans, picked over and soaked overnight

2 tbsp vegetable oil

1 large onion, chopped

2 garlic cloves, minced

1 tsp fresh ginger, grated

1 tsp ground coriander

¼ tsp ground cardamom

1 tsp fennel seed

½ tsp dried thyme

1 tsp dried oregano

2 tbsp chilli powder

450 ml/¾ pt tomato juice

175-g/6-oz can tomato purée

1–2 tsp salt

Tabasco sauce to taste

Bredie

*B*redie is a South African stew of mutton, tomato juice and dried spotted beans similar to pinto beans. Its exotic combination of seasonings – cardamom, fennel and ginger – also includes some form of chillies. This version, made with lamb shanks, is mildly spicy, but can be made hotter with Tabasco sauce.

● Put the lamb shanks and bay leaves in a stockpot and cover with water. Bring to the boil, reduce heat and simmer for 45 minutes. Drain the beans and add to the lamb. Add enough water to cover by 2.5 cm/1 in. Return to the boil, reduce heat and simmer for 30 minutes. Remove the lamb shanks and let cool slightly while you prepare the other ingredients.

● Heat the oil in a large frying pan and sauté the onion and garlic for 2 minutes. Add the ginger, coriander, cardamom, fennel seed, thyme and oregano, and sauté for 5 minutes longer. Add to the beans. Add the chilli powder, tomato juice and tomato purée to the beans. Return to the boil, reduce heat and continue simmering, stirring occasionally and adding water if needed.

● When the lamb has cooled enough to handle, cut the meat and fat from the bones. Discard the fat and bones. Shred the meat and add it to the beans. When the beans are tender – about 1½ hours total cooking time – add salt and Tabasco to taste.

◀ *Bredie*

Michelle's Green Chilli Stew with Pork

MAKES 6 SERVINGS

Michelle Murray and I grew up baking chocolate chip cookies together in Los Angeles. Later, I moved to Florida and Michelle moved to New Mexico, where she makes this delicious baked stew of pork, potatoes, and roasted green chillies. The stew's heat depends on the type of green chillies used. For a hot dish, add several unseeded jalapeños or serrano chillies.

● Roast the chillies under the grill, turning, until all sides are blistered and charred but not yet solidly black. Remove the chillies and seal them in a paper bag or a covered dish. Let the chillies steam while you prepare the stew.

● Preheat the oven to 180°C/350°F/Gas Mark 4. In a dutch oven or large ovenproof pot, heat 2 tablespoons of the oil. Add the pork and cook, turning occasionally, until the meat is browned on all sides. Remove the pork with a slotted spoon and set aside. Discard liquids. Add the remaining oil to the pot and sauté the onion and garlic for

5 minutes. Put the pork back in the pan with the herbs, salt, stock, tomato sauce and tomatoes. Bring to the boil, cover and place in the oven.

● Peel, seed and chop the roasted green chillies. Chop the jalapeños or serranos if you are using them. After the stew has baked for 30 minutes, add the chillies and potatoes. Cover and return to the oven. Cook until the meat is tender and potatoes are done, about 1 hour. There should be ample liquid, but check once or twice during baking, and add beef stock if needed.

ingredients

- **8 Anaheim, poblano, or green New Mexico chillies, or a combination**
- **4 tbsp vegetable oil**
- **900 g/2 lb pork, cut into 4-cm/1½-in chunks**
- **1½ medium onions, chopped**
- **3 garlic cloves, minced**
- **2 tsp dried oregano**
- **½ tsp dried rosemary**
- **1 tsp salt**
- **750 ml/1¼ pt beef stock**
- **250-ml/8-fl oz can tomato sauce**
- **425-g/15-oz can tomatoes, chopped**
- **2–3 jalapeño or serrano chillies, unseeded and minced, optional**
- **3–4 medium potatoes, peeled and cut into 2.5-cm/1-in chunks**

Hoppin' John with Smoked Turkey

350 g/12 oz dried black-eyed peas, picked over and soaked overnight

150 g/5 oz smoked turkey, chopped

1 tbsp chilli powder

1 tsp ground cumin

2 Tbsp, olive oil

1 large onion, chopped

1 celery stick, chopped

3 garlic cloves, minced

3 jalapeño chillies, unseeded and minced

2 medium tomatoes, seeded and chopped

4 spring onions, chopped

2 tbsp fresh coriander, chopped

about 2 tsp salt

625 g/1½ lb cooked white rice

Hoppin' John is spicy black-eyed peas served over rice. It is a Southern dish traditionally eaten on New Year's Day, when it is supposed to bring good luck for the coming year. It is usually flavoured with pork, but this recipe uses smoked turkey and lots of chilli. If a turkey bone is available, throw it into the pan while the beans are simmering.

● Drain the black-eyed peas, put them in a stockpot and add enough water to cover by 5 cm/2 in. Add the turkey meat and, if available, a turkey bone. Add the chilli powder and cumin and bring to the boil, reduce heat and simmer.

● Heat the olive oil in a frying pan and sauté the onion, celery, garlic and one of the minced chillies for 5 minutes, then add to the peas. Continue simmering until the peas are tender, about 1½ hours.

● When the peas are tender, add the remaining chillies, the tomatoes, spring onions and coriander. Add salt, taste, and adjust seasonings. Simmer for 2 minutes, then ladle over the bowls of rice.

Pozole

Pozole, a main-course stew of pork, hominy and chillies, originated in the Mexican state of Jalisco and was adopted by the American Indians of the South West. This version begins with a homemade stock of pork and chicken. Pozole is usually eaten with shredded lettuce, chopped radishes and cucumber.

ingredients

1 large onion, cut into chunks

3 garlic cloves, minced

1 celery stick, cut into several pieces

900 g/2 lb pork neck bones

900 g/2 lb chicken backs, necks, wings

3 tbsp vegetable oil

1.4 kg/3 lb pork, cubed

6 large dried chillies, such as ancho or New Mexico

2 tsp dried oregano

2 tsp ground cumin

750 ml/1¼ pt canned hominy

2 tbsp fresh coriander, chopped

1–2 tsp salt

● Put the onion, garlic, celery, pork bones and chicken pieces in a large stockpot and add water. Bring to the boil, then reduce heat and simmer, uncovered, for 2 hours. Pour through a wire sieve, skim fat and return the stock to the heat. You should have at least 1.75 l/3 pt stock. If not, add enough water to equal 1.75 l/3 pt. When the bones have cooled slightly, remove any meat and return it to the stock. Discard the fat, bones and strained solids.

● Heat the oil in a large saucepan and cook the cubed pork until lightly browned. Add the pork to the stock.

● Remove the stems and seeds from the dried chillies. Cut each chilli in several pieces and put in a narrow, deep bowl. Pour 250 ml/8 fl oz boiling water over the chillies and let stand for 30 minutes. Purée the chillies and soaking liquid in a blender or food processor to form a smooth sauce. Strain the sauce and discard the solids. Add the sauce to the pork.

● Add the oregano and cumin to the stew. When the pork has simmered for at least 1 hour, add the hominy and coriander. Cook for 15 minutes. Add salt, taste, and adjust seasonings.

6

VEGETARIAN CHILLI

There is no such dish as vegetarian chilli. It's an oxymoron. Chilli, by definition, has meat as a primary ingredient. But many vegetarians love chilli and have spent hours concocting alternatives to the traditional meaty stew. Typically, one or more types of beans are the backbone of a vegetarian chilli – and if you're looking for weird chilli ingredients, this is where you will find them. Here are seven recipes for vegetarian chilli that include tofu, bulgur, goat's cheese, peaches and a startling array of vegetables.

Vegetarian Black Bean Chilli

Two kinds of chillies plus chilli powder make this a pleasantly spicy dish, while fresh coriander and spring onions added at the end add texture. Feta cheese sprinkled on top gives a nice finishing touch.

ingredients

350 g/12 oz dried black beans, picked over and soaked

1 bay leaf

2 ancho chillies

2 tbsp vegetable oil

3 medium onions, chopped

2 celery sticks, chopped

3 garlic cloves, minced

2 tsp ground cumin

2 tsp dried oregano

1 tbsp chilli powder

2 u 400-g/14-oz cans tomatoes, chopped

1 canned chipotle chilli, minced

about 2 tsp salt

100 g/4 oz spring onions, chopped

15 g/½ oz fresh coriander, chopped

1 tbsp balsamic vinegar

about 100 g/4 oz feta cheese, crumbled

● Drain and rinse the beans. Put them in a large pot and cover with fresh water. Add the bay leaf and bring to the boil. Reduce the heat and simmer the beans while you prepare the other ingredients, adding water if needed.

● Remove the stems and seeds from the ancho chillies. Place the anchos in a small, heatproof bowl, pour 175 ml/6 fl oz boiling water over them and stir so they are covered. Let them soften in the hot water for about 30 minutes.

● Heat the oil in a large frying pan and sauté the onion and celery until the celery is soft, 6–8 minutes. (Do this in two batches if you don't have a very large pan.) Add the garlic, cumin, oregano and chilli powder and sauté for 1 minute longer. Add the mixture to the beans.

● Put the softened ancho chillies and their soaking water in a blender or food processor. Add about 100 g/4 oz of the chopped tomatoes and the chipotle chilli. Purée until smooth. Add the chilli mixture to the beans along with the remaining tomatoes. Continue simmering the beans until tender, 1¼–1½ hours total. Add salt and adjust to taste. Add the spring onions, coriander and vinegar and cook about 2 minutes. Ladle into bowls and sprinkle feta cheese over top.

Robin's Vegetarian Chilli with Peaches and Three Beans

MAKES 12 SERVINGS

Robin Benedick isn't a vegetarian, but she's always looking for meatless dishes. In Orlando, Florida, she found a restaurant that made an unusual vegetarian chilli sweetened by peaches – this is her version. Although she likes spicy food, she suggests starting with small amounts of cayenne and Tabasco sauce, then adding more if you want a hotter chilli. Use the liquid from the canned tomatoes, and some of the liquid from the beans. Robin doesn't add salt to her chilli, but you may wish to add salt if the beans are unsalted.

● Put all the ingredients, except the beans, in a stockpot with about 250 ml/ 8 fl oz water and stir well. Bring to the boil, reduce heat and simmer for 30 minutes, stirring often to avoid scorching, and adding water if needed.

● After 30 minutes, add the beans and enough liquid for the desired consistency. Simmer for 15 minutes more. Taste and adjust seasonings.

ingredients

1 red pepper, coarsely chopped

2 green peppers, coarsely chopped

1 large onion, coarsely chopped

1 peach, peeled and coarsely chopped

2 u 400-g/14-oz cans tomatoes, coarsely chopped

2 u 400-g/14-oz cans tomato sauce

1 tsp Tabasco sauce

¼ tsp dried thyme

1 tsp dried oregano

2 tsp ground cumin, or more to taste

1 tbsp chilli powder

1 tsp black pepper

2 u 300-g/10-oz cans cannellini beans

2 T 400-g/1-lb cans black beans

450-g/1-lb can kidney beans

Lentil and Vegetable Chilli

MAKES 4 TO 6 SERVINGS

This vegetable stew combines kidney beans, lentils, peas and carrots to make a chunky, mildly spicy vegetarian chilli.

ingredients

175 g/6 oz dried kidney beans, picked over and soaked overnight

1 bay leaf

1 tbsp vegetable oil

1 celery stick, chopped

1 medium onion, chopped

1 clove garlic, minced

2 tsp chilli powder

½ tsp dried oregano

½ tsp dried basil

400-g/14-oz can tomatoes, chopped

50 g/2 oz lentils

100 g/4 oz sliced carrots

100 g/4 oz peas, fresh or frozen

about 1 tsp salt

● Drain the beans, put them in a large saucepan and cover with fresh water. Add the bay leaf. Bring to the boil, reduce the heat and simmer. Heat the oil in a frying pan and sauté the celery and onion for 5 minutes. Add the garlic and sauté for 1 minute. Add the vegetables to the beans, along with the chilli powder, oregano, basil, and tomatoes. Return to the boil, reduce heat and simmer, adding water if needed.

● After the beans have cooked for 1 hour, add the lentils. (Lentil cooking times vary, depending on how they were processed. If the cooking instructions on the packet are more or less than 20 minutes, adjust the time you add them to the chilli so that they are done about 5 minutes before the chilli is ready.) Wait for 10 minutes, add water if necessary, then add the carrots. After 5 minutes, add the peas. Cook for 10 minutes, add salt and adjust seasonings to taste.

▶ *Lentil and Vegetable Chilli*

Angela's Vegetarian Chilli

MAKES 6 SERVINGS

This chilli started with a beefy recipe from Campbell's Soup, but Angela Bradbery kept fiddling with it until she got the chilli she wanted – no meat, lots of beans and vegetables, not quite so sweet. She uses both hot pepper sauce and cayenne to taste, so the dish is as mild or as spicy as you want.

ingredients

1 tbsp vegetable oil

1 onion, chopped

1 green pepper, chopped

2 garlic cloves, minced

1 can condensed Tomato Rice Soup

450-g/1-lb can tomatoes, including juice, chopped

175-g/6-oz can tomato purée

450-g/1-lb can corn

4 tbsp chilli powder

2 T 450-g/1-lb cans kidney beans

ketchup to taste

hot pepper sauce

cayenne

● Heat the oil in a frying pan and sauté the onion, green pepper, and garlic for 5 minutes. Put the vegetables in a large saucepan with the soup, tomatoes, tomato purée, corn and chilli powder. Stir well and add 250 ml/8 fl oz water or so for a soupy consistency. Add the kidney beans, plus the ketchup, hot pepper sauce and cayenne to taste. Bring to the boil, reduce the heat and simmer for 30 minutes.

Vegetarian Chilli with Tofu

This is a thick, tomatoey chilli with fried bits of tofu. Its hotness depends on the type of dried chillies used.

ingredients

12 oz firm tofu

6 dried Anaheim, ancho, pasilla, or New Mexico chillies, or a combination

about 4 tbsp vegetable oil

1 large onion, chopped

1 green pepper, chopped

2 celery sticks, chopped

4 garlic cloves, minced

450 ml/¾ pt vegetable stock

250 ml/8 fl oz tomato sauce

425-g/15-oz can tomatoes, chopped

1 tsp ground cumin

1 tsp ground coriander

2 tsp dried oregano

1 tsp paprika

15 g/½ oz fresh coriander, chopped

about 1 tsp salt

● If not using pressed tofu, it should be pressed to remove excess water. Place the tofu on a plate, put another plate on top and weight it with cans or other heavy objects. Tofu should be pressed for at least 30 minutes before using.

● Split the dried chillies in half and remove the stems and seeds. Put the pieces in a small heatproof bowl and pour 250 ml/8 fl oz boiling water over the chillies. Let them steep in the water for 30 minutes, stirring occasionally to be sure all parts of the chillies are covered with water.

● Heat 2 tablespoons of the oil in a large frying pan and sauté the onion, green pepper, celery, and garlic for 5 minutes. Put the sautéed vegetables in a large pan with the stock, tomato sauce, tomatoes and seasonings. Bring to the boil, reduce heat and simmer.

● After the chillies have soaked for 30 minutes, pour the chillies and the soaking liquid into a blender or food processor. Purée until a smooth sauce is formed. Strain the sauce to remove seeds and bits of skin, discard solids. Add the strained sauce to the simmering sauce.

● Discard the liquids from the tofu. Cut the tofu into 5-mm/¼-in cubes. Heat the remaining oil in a frying pan and fry the tofu over medium-high, turning once, until tofu is slightly browned, 2–3 minutes a side. Add the tofu to the chilli. Let the chilli simmer for 30 minutes. Add the coriander and salt, taste and adjust seasonings.

Vegetarian Chilli with Corn and Bulgur

ingredients

175 g/6 oz dried kidney beans, picked over and soaked overnight

450 ml/¾ pt vegetable stock

2 tbsp vegetable oil

1½ medium onions, chopped

½ green pepper, chopped

3 garlic cloves, minced

1 carrot, peeled and coarsely chopped

425-g/15-oz can tomatoes, chopped

175-ml/6-fl oz can tomato purée

2 tbsp chilli powder

2 tbsp hot or Mexican chilli powder

1 tsp ground cumin

1 tsp dried oregano

40 g/1½ oz bulgur

200 g/7 oz corn, fresh or frozen

150-g/5-oz can black olives, sliced

salt to taste

This pleasantly spicy chilli, with corn and olives, may remind you of old-fashioned tamale pie. It is thickened with bulgur, a partially cooked cracked wheat available in health-food shops.

● Drain the kidney beans, put in large pan and add just enough water to cover. Add 250 ml/8 fl oz of the vegetable stock. Bring to the boil, reduce heat and simmer.

● Heat the oil in a large frying pan and sauté the onion, green pepper, and garlic for 5 minutes. Add to the beans with the carrot, tomatoes, tomato purée and spices. Stir and continue simmering.

● After the beans have simmered for about 45 minutes, put the remaining vegetable stock in a small pan and bring to the boil. Add the bulgur, stir well, and boil for 5 minutes. Remove from the heat and let stand for 10 minutes. Add the bulgur and stock to the chilli. Add the corn and continue cooking, stirring often and adding water if needed, until the beans are tender, about 30 minutes (about 1½ hours total). Stir in the olives. Taste, add salt if needed and adjust seasonings.

Three-bean Vegetarian Chilli

MAKES 6 TO 8 SERVINGS

This mildly spicy chilli starts with a base of three beans – black beans, pinquitos and chick peas. It gets its flavour from three kinds of chillies and three forms of tomatoes, including sun-dried tomatoes, which provide bits of tart, chewy surprise.

● The night before: pick over the three types of beans for stones or other debris. Put all the beans in a big bowl or pan, fill with water and let soak overnight.

● After the beans have soaked at least 8 hours, drain them, rinse and drain again. Put them in a large pan and add enough water to cover by 5 cm/2 in. Bring to the boil, reduce heat and simmer.

● Heat the oil in a frying pan and sauté the onion, celery and garlic for 5 minutes. Add to the beans with the tomatoes and tomato sauce.

● Roast the chillies under the grill, turning, until all sides are blistered and nearly blackened. Remove from the grill and put in a paper bag or covered bowl to steam.

● Add the chilli powder to the chilli. In a small, dry frying pan, heat the cumin seeds, oregano and basil, shaking frequently, until they are toasted. Remove from the heat and let cool slightly. Grind in a grinder or pestle and mortar, or put between two pieces of waxed paper and crush with the end of a rolling pin. Add to the chilli.

● Peel the roasted chillies and remove the stems and seeds. Chop the chillies and add them to the chilli.

● Simmer, stirring occasionally and adding water if needed, until the beans are tender, 1½ to 2 hours. About 10 minutes before the chilli is done, add the chopped jalapeño and salt. Taste and adjust seasonings. Stir in the coriander immediately before serving.

ingredients

100 g/4 oz dried black beans

100 g/4 oz dried pinquitos

100 g/4 oz dried chick peas

2 tbsp vegetable oil

1 large onion, chopped

2 celery sticks, chopped

4 garlic cloves, minced

425-g/15-oz can tomatoes, chopped

250-ml/8-fl oz can tomato sauce

4 Anaheim or poblano chillies, or a combination

2 tbsp chilli powder

2 tsp cumin seeds

2 tsp dried oregano

1 tsp dried basil

1 jalapeño chilli, unseeded, minced

1–2 tsp salt

15 g/½ oz fresh coriander, chopped

7

CHILLI AS AN INGREDIENT

You won't hear any of these wine-tasting adjectives – subtle, impudent, delicate – applied to chilli. Chilli is hearty and powerful. If you find a chilli-lover searching for an adjective, it is usually a search for some variation of hot – fiery, incendiary, a killer. Even in small quantities, chilli dominates a dish, even then it's delicious. Here are six ways to use chillies as an ingredient, from the sauce on chilli dogs to the filling in tamale pie.

Chilli for Chilli Dogs and Chilli Burgers

ingredients

450 g/1 lb ground beef

1 small onion, finely chopped

2 garlic cloves, minced

250 ml/8 fl oz canned enchilada sauce

½ tsp ground cumin

½ tsp dried marjoram

about 120 ml/4 fl oz water

Canned enchilada sauce provides the flavouring for this chilli, a thick sauce for spooning over hot dogs and hamburgers. The chilli's heat will depend on the type of enchilada sauce, but can be made hotter by adding cayenne or hot pepper sauce.

● In a large frying pan, brown the meat, chopping it finely as it cooks. Add the onion and garlic and cook for 5 minutes. Drain and discard fat. Add the enchilada sauce, cumin and marjoram. Add sufficient water to make the sauce slightly watery – it will reduce and thicken as it cooks. Cook over low heat for about 15 minutes, or until the sauce is of the desired consistency.

Alma Cherry's Chilli Sauce

ingredients

450 g/1 lb hamburger steak

250 ml/8 fl oz ketchup

1 small onion, finely chopped

2 celery sticks, finely chopped

½ tsp salt

chilli powder to taste

Half a century ago, Alma Cherry was determined to duplicate the chilli sauce served at the family's favourite restaurant in southern Indiana. When the cook refused to divulge the secrets of the popular sauce to any of the customers, Alma pestered the local grocer until he told her what supplies the cook bought. Then she experimented with quantities until she was happy with the sauce, which she uses to make chilli dogs. The recipe was given to me by her son, Alan, one of my co-workers. It is a mild sauce, with the celery adding a hint of sweetness.

● Cook the hamburger steak until browned. Spoon off and discard the fat. Add the ketchup and 250 ml/8 fl oz water and mix well. Add the onion and celery and cook until soft, about 10 minutes. Add the salt and chilli powder to taste. Cook, stirring frequently, until the sauce is thick.

▶ *Chilli for Chilli Dogs and Chilli Burgers*

Chilli Pie

ingredients

625 g/1½ lb chilli

100 g/4 oz corn chips

½ medium onion, chopped

225 g/8 oz Cheddar cheese, grated

*A*lso known as Frito Pie, this simple casserole of corn chips, chilli, onion and cheese is a favourite with kids. Use your choice of chilli, with or without beans, but it should be a little soupy, not dry. Bake it in a 25-cm/10-in springform tin or 1.75-l/3-pt casserole.

● Preheat the oven to 180°C/350°F/Gas Mark 4. Heat the chilli until it bubbles. Spread about two-thirds of the corn chips in the bottom of the baking tin. Pour the hot chilli over the chips. Sprinkle the onions, then the cheese over the chilli, then top with the remaining chips. Bake for 25 minutes.

Tamale Pie

ingredients

½ tsp salt

¼ tsp ground cumin

1 tsp chilli powder

150 g/5 oz cornmeal

625 g/1½ lb cooked chilli

450-g/1-lb can corn

150-g/5-oz can olives, sliced

225 g/8 oz Cheddar cheese grated

*T*his homely dish is an all-American casserole based on Mexican tamales. In this version, the chilli is mixed with corn and olives, poured into a cornmeal crust, topped with cheese and baked. A beanless, ground meat chilli such as Rapid Fire Chilli (page 20) is traditional, but you can also use chilli with diced meat. You will need a 25-cm/10-in springform tin, or 1.6-l/2¾-pt or larger casserole.

● Preheat the oven to 180°C/350°F/Gas Mark 4. Spray a baking tin or casserole with non-stick spray.
● Bring 450 ml/¾ pt water to the boil in a large saucepan. Mix the salt, cumin and chilli powder and set aside. Mix the cornmeal and 250 ml/8 fl oz cold water to form a thin, smooth paste. Slowly stir the cornmeal paste into the boiling water, stirring constantly. Reduce the heat to low, add the spice mix and continue stirring until the water is absorbed and the mixture is a thick mush. Remove from heat and let cool slightly. Spread the cornmeal over the bottom and up the sides of the baking tin to form a crust. Let it cool while you prepare the filling.
● Mix the chilli with the corn and olives, and reheat. The mixture should be thick, more like a paste than a stew. If the chilli is soupy, mix 2 tablespoons cornmeal with 2 tablespoons cold water to form a

▲ *Tamale Pie*

paste, then mix the paste into the chilli.
Cook a few minutes until it is thick.

● Pour the chilli into the crust. Sprinkle
the grated cheese over the top. Bake for
30 minutes. Serve hot.

Chilli Bean Sauce

MAKES 6 TO 8 SERVINGS

This mixture of pre-cooked pinto beans and chilli made with ground beef is a versatile and easy-to-make mixture. It makes a thick sauce that can be spooned over burgers and hot dogs. Or add corn chips, Cheddar cheese and chopped onions, and eat it by the bowlful. The chilli is moderately hot with 1 teaspoon chilli flakes.

ingredients

1 tsp vegetable oil

1 medium onion, chopped

2 garlic cloves, minced

450 g/1 lb ground beef

450 ml/¾ pt beef stock

3 tbsp chilli powder

2 tsp ground cumin

1–2 tsp crushed red chilli flakes

450-g/1-lb can pre-cooked pinto beans

about ½ tsp salt

● Heat the oil in a frying pan and sauté the onion and garlic for 5 minutes. Remove the vegetables and set aside. Cook the ground beef in the pan until browned. Drain off excess fat. Put the onion and beef in a large saucepan with the beef stock, stir well. Bring the mixture to the boil, reduce heat. Add the chilli powder, cumin and 1 teaspoon chilli flakes.

● Simmer, adding water if needed, until the meat is falling apart, 45–60 minutes. The mixture should be a little soupy. Stir in the beans and cook for 5 minutes. Taste, add salt and additional chilli flakes if desired.

Chilli Salad

MAKES 6 SERVINGS

This is a salad that children will love – layers of chilli, cheese and corn chips disguising the vegetables. A ground-meat chilli with beans is preferred, but most chillies will do.

ingredients

1 head iceberg lettuce, torn into pieces

450 g/1 lb chilli, heated

75 g/3 oz spring onions, chopped

225 g/8 oz Cheddar cheese, grated

50-g/2-oz can olives, sliced

2–3 tomatoes, cut into wedges

1 large or 2 small avocados, peeled and cut into wedges

75–100 g/3–4 oz corn chips

● Divide the lettuce among six serving plates. Spoon 120 ml/4 fl oz of the hot chilli over each. Sprinkle the spring onions, cheese and olives over the chilli. Divide the tomato and avocado wedges among the plates, then top with corn chips.

▶ *Chilli Salad*

CHILLI
ACCOMPANIMENTS

Even the most passionate chillihead wants something besides chilli in his diet. There are certain dishes that always marry well with chilli – beans, cornbread, cole slaw. Following are 18 recipes for foods to be served with chilli – five kinds of beans, three kinds of cornbread, plus salads, breads, and dips.

Smoky Black Beans

Smoky barbecue sauce adds flavour to these spicy black beans.

350 g/12 oz black beans, picked over and soaked overnight

1 large onion, chopped

1 tbsp smoky barbecue sauce

2 tsp chilli powder

½ tsp cayenne

1 large tomato, chopped

15 g/½ oz fresh coriander, chopped

2–3 tsp salt

● Drain the beans, put them in a large saucepan with the chopped onion and cover with water. Bring the beans to the boil, reduce heat and simmer for 1½–2 hours, adding water if needed.

● About 30 minutes before the beans are done, add the sauce, chilli powder, and cayenne. When the beans are ready, add the tomato and coriander and cook for 2 minutes longer. Add salt, taste and adjust seasonings.

Hot Black Beans

Chilli flakes – hot red chillies that are dried and crushed – add plenty of heat to this bean dish.

300 g/12 oz black beans, picked over and soaked overnight

1 large onion, chopped

2 tbsp chilli flakes

1 tsp ground cumin

3 garlic cloves, minced

2–3 tsp salt

1 large tomato, seeded and diced

● Drain the beans, put them in a large saucepan with the chopped onion and cover with water. Bring to the boil, reduce heat and simmer for 1½–2 hours, adding water if needed.

● About 30 minutes before the beans are cooked, add the chilli flakes, cumin, and garlic. When the beans are ready, add the salt and tomato. Taste and adjust seasonings.

▶ *Smoky Black Beans*

Pinto Beans and Ham Hocks

Smoked ham hocks lend their smoky flavour to these beans. The beans can be served as a side dish but make a substantial dish on their own. If you wish, chop the meat from the ham hocks and add it to the beans just before serving. The beans are hot, but the heat can be reduced by removing the veins and seeds from the jalapeños.

ingredients

350 g/12 oz pinto beans, picked over and soaked overnight

1 large or 2 small smoked ham hocks

1 large onion, chopped

3 garlic cloves, minced

2 jalapeño chillies, unseeded and minced

75 g/3 oz spring onions, finely chopped

15 g/½ oz fresh coriander, chopped

2–3 tsp salt

● Drain the beans, put in a pot with the ham hocks, onion and garlic and add enough water to cover. Bring to the boil, reduce heat and simmer for at least 1½ hours, adding water if needed. Add the jalapeños about 15 minutes before serving. When the beans are cooked, add the spring onions, coriander, and salt to taste.

Drunken Beans

Simmered in beer, these beans are pleasantly spicy with a hint of cumin.

ingredients

350 g/12 oz pinto beans, picked over and soaked overnight

1 large onion, chopped

4 chillies de arbol, broken in half

350 ml/12 fl oz dark Mexican beer

½ tsp ground cumin

1 large tomato, peeled and chopped

2 tbsp fresh coriander, chopped

about 1 tbsp salt

● Put the beans, onion and chillies in a large saucepan and add enough cold water to barely cover them. Add the beer and cumin. Bring to the boil, reduce heat and simmer for at least 1½ hours. About 10 minutes before serving, add the tomato and coriander. Add salt to taste.

▶ *Drunken Beans*

ingredients

1 or 2 ham hocks

2 bay leaves

2 tbsp vegetable oil

1 large onion, chopped

4 garlic cloves, minced

1 celery stick, finely chopped

350 g/12 oz red beans, picked over and soaked overnight

2 carrots, peeled and finely chopped

250-ml/8-fl oz can tomato sauce

1 large or 2 small tomatoes, chopped (can be canned tomatoes)

2–3 jalapeño or serrano chillies

1 tbsp chilli powder

½ tsp ground cumin

425-g/15-oz can chick peas

2–3 tsp salt

Spicy Basque Beans

MAKES 8 TO 10 SIDE DISH SERVINGS

*O*ne of the ethnic groups that influenced the cuisine of the West Coast was Basque shepherds, who came to the inland valleys of California, Oregon and Washington, as well as Idaho and Nevada in the 19th century. These beans might be served as a side dish at a Basque barbecue, but they can also be eaten as a light main dish. For a hot dish, leave the chilli seeds and veins intact; remove them for a milder dish.

● Put the ham hocks and bay leaves in a large pot and add enough water to cover by 5 cm/2 in. Bring to the boil, reduce heat and simmer for 30 minutes. While the ham hocks are simmering, cook the vegetables. Heat the oil in a large frying pan and sauté the onion, garlic and celery for 5 minutes. Drain the red beans.

● Add the sautéed vegetables and beans to the ham hocks. Add water to cover if needed. Bring to the boil, reduce heat and simmer for another 30 minutes. Remove the ham hocks from the beans and let them cool for about 15 minutes. Meanwhile, add the remaining ingredients, except the chick peas and salt, to the beans.

● When the ham hocks are cool enough to handle, cut the meat and fat from the bones. Discard the fat and bones. Shred the meat and add it to the beans.

● Cook the beans until they are tender, adding water if needed, a total of about 1½ hours. Add the check peas. Taste, add salt and adjust seasonings. Cook for about 10 minutes longer.

Mexican Corn Muffins

MAKES 16 TO 20 MUFFINS

*S*tudded with corn and jalapeño chillies and flavoured with Cheddar cheese, these muffins complement any chilli.

● Preheat the oven to 190°C/375°F/Gas Mark 5. Lightly grease or spray muffin tins. Combine the cornmeal, flour, salt, baking powder, bicarbonate of soda and sugar in a large bowl.

● In a small bowl, lightly beat the eggs with a fork. Mix the melted butter and buttermilk, and pour into the eggs. Stir in the corn and chillies. Pour the liquids into the dry ingredients and beat by hand until the batter is mixed. Stir in the cheese. Pour the batter into the muffin tins, filling them to just below the rim. Bake 25–30 minutes, until golden.

ingredients

175 g/6 oz cornmeal

50 g/2 oz plain flour

1 tsp salt

2 tsp baking powder

1 tsp bicarbonate soda

1 tbsp sugar

3 eggs

100 g/4 oz melted butter

250 ml/8 fl oz buttermilk

425-g/15-oz can cream-style corn

6 jalapeño chillies, seeded and chopped

225 g/8 oz Cheddar cheese, grated

Skillet Cornbread with Bacon and Jalapeños

MAKES 8 SERVINGS

ingredients

4 rashers bacon

325 g/11oz cornmeal

75 g/3 oz plain flour

1½ tsp salt

1 tbsp baking powder

2 tbsp sugar

2 eggs, lightly beaten

400 ml/16 fl oz milk

100 g/4 oz melted butter, or butter and bacon fat

4 jalapeño chillies, seeded and minced

With a dense texture and minimal sugar, this is a traditional cornbread, but for the addition of jalapeño chillies. It is baked in a sizzling-hot frying pan, and seasoned with bacon fat and bits of fried bacon, much like old-fashioned cracklin' cornbread. A heavy, 23-cm/9-in or 25-cm/10-in cast-iron frying pan is required.

● Preheat the oven to 220°C/425°F/Gas Mark 7. Fry the bacon until crisp in a cast-iron frying pan. Remove the bacon and drain on paper towels. When the bacon is cool enough to handle, crumble it. Save about 1 tablespoon bacon fat for the pan. Discard the rest, or combine with melted butter to make 120 ml/4 fl oz fat. Combine the dry ingredients.

● Brush bacon fat around the bottom and up the sides of the frying pan so it is completely oiled. Put the pan in the oven to heat.

● In a separate bowl, lightly beat the eggs with a fork. Combine the milk and melted butter or butter/bacon fat combination, then add to the eggs. Stir in the chillies. Pour the liquids into the dry ingredients and stir by hand until the batter is well-mixed. Stir in the crumbled bacon.

● The frying pan should be very hot and the bacon fat just short of smoking. Carefully pour the batter into the pan. It will sizzle as it hits the fat. Bake until the cornbread is golden brown, 35–40 minutes. Let cool slightly, then cut into wedges. Serve warm.

Light, Sweet Cornbread

Most chilli aficionados prefer a dense cornbread with no sweetening and a low proportion of flour. This recipe is for those who like a light, sweet cornbread.

ingredients

200 g/7 oz plain flour

150 g/5 oz cornmeal

100 g/4 oz sugar

2 tsp baking powder

1 tsp bicarbonate of soda

1 tsp salt

2 eggs

350 ml/12 fl oz buttermilk

100 g/4 oz melted butter

● Preheat the oven to 180°C/350°F/Gas Mark 4. Spray or lightly butter an 8-inch square baking tin. Mix the dry ingredients in a large bowl.

● In a small bowl, lightly beat the eggs with a fork. Stir in the buttermilk, then the melted butter. Pour the liquids into the dry ingredients and beat the batter by hand until well-blended. Pour the batter into the baking tin. Bake until the cornbread is golden brown, 35–40 minutes. Cool slightly before cutting into nine squares.

Chilli Con Queso

Chile con queso is a sort of South Western fondue – melted cheese with chillies, onions, garlic and tomatoes. It is a terrific dip for chips, crackers or crudités, or can be a main dish fondue, served with chunks of bread. It can be kept warm by setting the pot over a candle or on a warming tray. For a mild dip, remove the seeds and veins from the jalapeños.

ingredients

25 g/1 oz butter

2–3 jalapeño chillies, minced

1 garlic clove, minced

1 medium tomato, seeded and chopped

3 spring onions, minced

450 g/1 lb Cheddar cheese, grated

● Preheat the oven to 180°C/350°F/Gas Mark 4. Melt the butter in a frying pan and sauté the chillies, garlic, tomatoes and spring onions for 5 minutes. Continue cooking, if needed, until the liquids have evaporated.

● Stir the vegetables into the grated cheese in an ovenproof serving dish. Bake until the cheese is bubbling, about 12 minutes. Serve immediately.

▶ *Chilli Con Queso*

Navajo Fry Bread

MAKES 6 SERVINGS

Golden, puffy Navajo Fry Bread is a tradition of the American South West. It goes well with any chilli, but especially with green chilli stews.

ingredients

225 g/8 oz plain flour

1½ tsp baking powder

¾ tsp salt

25 g/1 oz non-fat dried milk

175 ml/6 fl oz water

vegetable oil or lard for frying

● Combine the dry ingredients together. Add the water and knead the dough until soft. Divide the dough into six equal pieces. Shape each piece into a round, then flatten each round to a thickness of 5–12 mm/¼–½ in. Poke a small hole in the centre of each.

● Pour oil or melt lard in a large frying pan or Dutch oven to a depth of 2.5 cm/1 in and heat to 190°C/375°F. Carefully drop one or two rounds of dough into the hot oil, keeping the rounds separated. Fry, turning once, until both sides are golden and puffy, about 1 minute a side. Remove, let drain for a few seconds. Serve hot.

Salsa Fresca

MAKES ABOUT 450 ML/¾ PT SALSA

Few extras accompany chilli as well as salsa and tortilla chips. Here is a recipe for a moderately hot fresh salsa that should be made no more than a few hours before it is to be eaten. The ingredients, especially the tomatoes, should be chopped by hand. A food processor will turn the tomatoes into pink mush. It's important that the tomatoes are ripe, or they will add little flavour to the salsa.

ingredients

300–450 g/11 oz–1 lb chopped tomatoes

½ medium red onion, finely chopped

2 jalapeño chillies, partly seeded, minced

1 garlic clove, minced

3–4 tbsp fresh coriander, chopped

2 tbsp fresh lime juice

1–2 tbsp olive oil

dash salt

● Combine all the ingredients together in a bowl. Let stand at least 30 minutes at room temperature before serving.

▶ *Navajo Fry Bread*

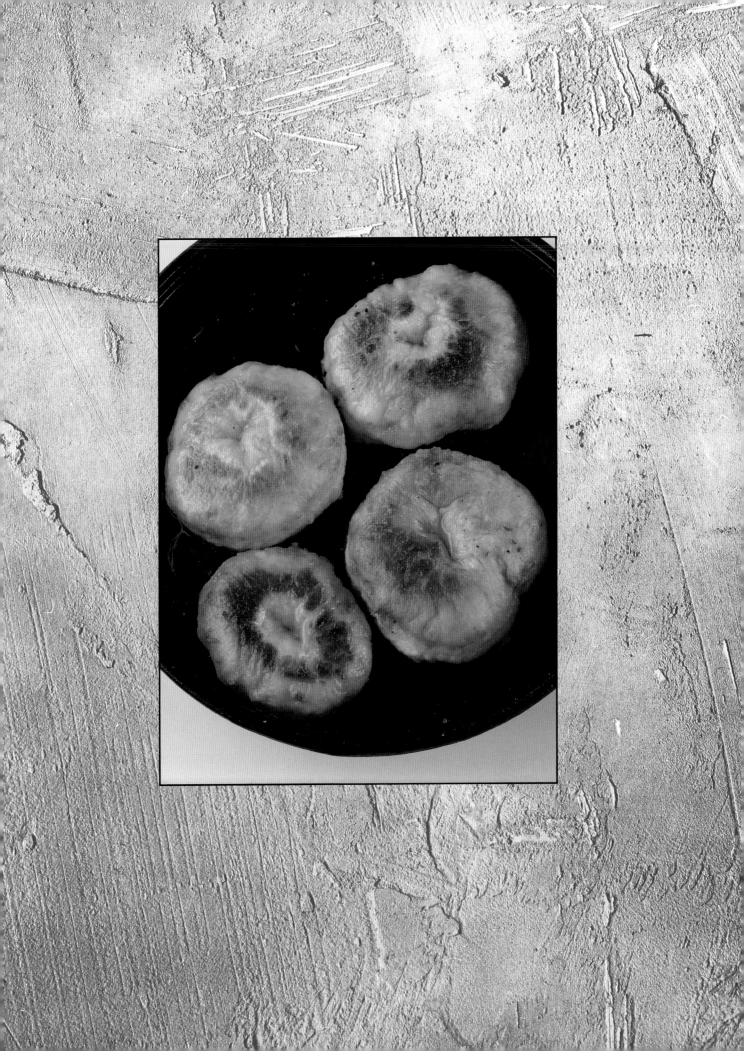

Avocado Salsa

MAKES ABOUT 500 ml/8 fl oz

ingredients

3 avocados diced

1 medium or 2 plum tomatoes, diced

½ medium red onion, finely chopped

2 jalapeño chillies, minced

3 tbsp fresh lime juice

1 tbsp olive oil

1 tbsp fresh coriander, chopped

pinch salt and black pepper

Avocado salsa is similar to guacamole, but the avocado is cubed rather than mashed, and is mixed with minced chillies. Use it as a dip for corn chips or a topping for chilli. If your avocados are slightly short of being perfectly ripe, add a little bottled avocado oil to improve the flavour of the salsa. If you mix the other ingredients in advance, don't dice the avocados until just before serving. Remove the seeds and veins from the jalapeño chillies for a milder salsa.

● Combine all the ingredients together in a bowl.

Karen's Jalapeño Breadsticks

*K*aren Nitkin was experimenting with no-fat recipes for her bread machine when she came across an odd one that used bananas instead of fat to make spicy breadsticks. The bananas didn't appeal to her, but the combination of garlic, jalapeño chillies and Parmesan cheese did, so she compromised a bit on the fat and came up with these. Extra-long and chewy, they are an excellent accompaniment to chilli.

FOR BREAD MACHINES:

● Combine the ingredients and place in the bread machine. Program the machine for dough. Remove the kneaded dough from the bread machine and leave in an oiled bowl for 20 minutes. Preheat the oven to 180°C/350°F/Gas Mark 4. Cut the dough into nine pieces. Roll each piece into a long stick on an unfloured surface. Bake for 20 minutes, until the sticks brown slightly. Let cool and serve.

BY HAND:

● Heat the water to 41–46°C/ 105–115°F. Add a pinch of flour and the yeast. Leave until the mixture develops a foamy head, about 10 minutes.

● While the yeast is proving, combine all the other ingredients, except the flours. Gradually stir in about half the flour. Turn the dough on to a lightly floured surface and knead in the remaining flour. Total kneading time should be 8–10 minutes. Place the dough in an oiled bowl, cover with a clean towel, and put in a warm place to rise for about 1½ hours. Knock back the dough, then leave for about 20 minutes. Preheat the oven to 180°C/350°F/Gas Mark 4. Cut the dough into nine pieces. Roll each piece into a long stick on an unfloured surface. Bake for 20 minutes, until the sticks brown slightly. Let cool and serve.

ingredients

175 g/6 oz strong flour

75 g/3 oz wholemeal flour

½ tsp salt

40 g/1½ oz yellow cornmeal

2 garlic cloves, minced

1 egg white

50 g/2 oz Parmesan cheese

2 jalapeño chillies, minced

150 ml/¼ pt water

4 tbsp vegetable oil

1½ tsp yeast

◄ *Avocado Salsa*

Coriander Chilli Dip

ingredients

3 tbsp fresh coriander, chopped

1 jalapeño chilli, seeded and minced

225 g/8 oz cream cheese, softened

175 g/6 g chilli, heated

3 spring onions, chopped

175 g/6 oz Cheddar cheese, grated

This cheesy layered dip should be served hot with tortilla chips and eaten quickly before the melted cheese hardens. Use a ground-meat chilli, with or without beans.

● Preheat the oven to 190°C/375°F/Gas Mark 5. With a wooden spoon, stir the coriander and chilli into the cream cheese. Spread the cream cheese over the bottom of a soufflé dish or small glass pie plate. Spread the chilli over the cream cheese. Sprinkle the spring onions over the chilli, and sprinkle the cheese over the top. Bake until the cheese is bubbly, about 12 minutes.

Hot Bean Dip

ingredients

450 g/1 lb cooked black beans

175 g/6 oz leftover chilli, heated

250 ml/8 fl oz salsa

1 tsp ground cumin

salt to taste

This easy party dip is made with black beans, leftover chilli and fresh or bottled salsa of your choice. Use California Five-way Chilli (page 79), Beef and Chorizo Chilli (page 36) or other chilli made with ground meat and no beans. You can use canned beans, but freshly cooked dried beans provide a better flavour and texture. The dip should be served hot with chips.

● Put all the ingredients in a blender or food processor. Purée in short bursts, using the pulse button, until the mixture is coarsely chopped, not smooth. Reheat the dip, taste, and adjust seasonings.

▶ *Tomato-cucumber Salad with Spicy Vinaigrette*

Tomato-cucumber Salad with Spicy Vinaigrette

MAKES 4 SERVINGS

Make this cooling salad several hours before serving so the vegetables absorb the flavours of the vinaigrette.

● Combine the olive oil, lime juice, vinegar, garlic, corinader, honey, hot pepper sauce, salt and pepper in a blender or food processor. Purée.

● Combine the tomatoes, cucumber and red onion. Toss with the dressing.

ingredients

5 tbsp olive oil

2 tbsp fresh lime juice

1 tbsp red wine vinegar

1 garlic clove, coarsely chopped

15 g/½ oz whole coriander leaves

1 tsp honey

few drops hot pepper sauce

pinch salt

pinch black pepper

4 beefsteak tomatoes, sliced

½ cucumber, peeled and thinly sliced

6 thin slices red onion, separated into rings

South Western Corn Salad
with Rajas

MAKES 6 SERVINGS

ingredients

4 tbsp olive oil

3 tbsp fresh lime juice

**2 tbsp fresh coriander,
finely chopped**

½ tsp ground cumin

1 garlic clove, minced

pinch salt

pinch pepper

1 poblano chilli

1 sweet red pepper

**575 g/1¼ lb corn, fresh
or frozen**

**½ green pepper, cut into
5-mm/¼-in dice**

**2 medium tomatoes,
seeded and chopped**

**⅓ medium red onion,
finely chopped**

**1 large avocado, peeled
and diced**

This corn salad is spicy but not hot and can be used as a relish with grilled meats. It is made with rajas, *strips of roasted chilli and red pepper. When possible, use fresh corn just cut from the cob, but frozen corn is acceptable. The salad is best when made several hours in advance so the flavours have a chance to blend, but not so long that it loses its crunch. If the salad is made in advance, the avocado should be cut and added just before serving.*

● Combine the olive oil, lime juice, coriander, cumin, garlic, salt and pepper, and shake well to make dressing. Set aside.

● Roast the chilli and red pepper under the grill, turning often, until all sides are charred, about 10 minutes. Remove and place in a paper bag or covered bowl. Leave to steam for at least 10 minutes.

● While the chilli and red pepper are cooling, cook the corn. Put the corn in a small pan with about 120 ml/4 fl oz water. Bring to the boil and cook for 5 minutes. Drain the corn and let it cool.

● Remove the chilli and pepper from the bag or bowl. Peel and discard the blackened skin, stems, and seeds. Cut the chilli and pepper into narrow strips.

● To make the salad, combine the corn, chilli and pepper strips, and remaining ingredients. Toss with the dressing. Taste and adjust seasonings.

▶ *Coleslaw*

Coleslaw

MAKES 6 TO 8 SERVINGS

*C*oleslaw is a traditional accompaniment to chilli, its tangy coolness offsetting the chilli's bite. For a more colourful slaw, substitute red cabbage for half the green cabbage. For variety, add dill or caraway seeds to the dressing. When possible, make the dressing a few hours in advance to allow the flavours to blend, then mix with the cabbage about 30 minutes before serving.

● Mix the cabbage and carrots in a large bowl. Combine the remaining ingredients and whisk to make a smooth dressing. Toss with the cabbage.

ingredients

1 small head cabbage, shredded

2 carrots, peeled and shredded

120 ml/4 fl oz buttermilk

175 ml/6 fl oz mayonnaise

2 tbsp cider vinegar

2 tbsp sugar

2 tsp celery seeds

1 tsp salt

1 tsp pepper

Index